SOCIAL WORK
AND
RECEIVED IDEAS

SOCIAL WORK AND RECEIVED IDEAS

CHRIS ROJEK,
GERALDINE PEACOCK
and STEWART COLLINS

ROUTLEDGE
London and New York

First published in 1988
by Routledge
11 New Fetter Lane, London EC4P 4EE
29 West 35th Street, New York, NY 10001

Typeset by Gilfillan Limited, Mitcham, Surrey.
Printed in Great Britain by
Billing & Sons Ltd, Worcester

British Library Cataloguing in Publication Data

Rojek, Chris
    Social work and received ideas.
    1. Welfare work. Theories
    I. Title II. Peacock, Geraldine
    III. Collins, Stewart
    361.3'01

ISBN 0-415-01274-0
ISBN 0-415-01275-9 Pbk.

Now when things go on from generation to generation in such a way that everyone takes over the concepts... then it happens only too easily that the concepts are gradually changed... they become like false coinage – while all the time all transactions happily continue to be carried out in them... Yet no one has any desire to undertake the business of revising the concepts.

Kierkegaard

Contents

Authors' note

The idea for this book was emphatically not 'received'. On the contrary, it was born in a Glasgow hostelry one early evening in autumn when we were two. Before the evening turned into the night we became three: a feat which none of us rightly recalls, but about which two of us harbour rotting suspicions.

In the beginning we approached our task in the spirit of practical social work. By the time we reached the middle, we were working hard to remain social. And by the final sentence, we were social, working, but resident and employed in different parts of the country.

Readers with a nose for nepotism may wonder at the connection between the imprint of the book and the current employment status of one of the authors. Such readers should know that the book was contracted, together with its companion volume, *The Haunt of Misery*, when all three authors worked as full-time lecturers at The Queen's College, Glasgow. Furthermore, the original publisher was to be Tavistock Publications, not Routledge. However, along the way, the market which dispersed the authors around the country also intervened to bring about the merger of Tavistock into Routledge. Such is the manner of the world and the times in which we live.

Introduction:
'Metaphysical subtleties and
theological niceties'

Social work is about people. It is also about words. The relationship between the two seems simple and obvious. However, as Marx (1977: 76) said of the commodity form under capitalism, 'its analysis shows that it is, in reality, a very queer thing abounding in metaphysical subtleties and theological niceties'. Undoubtedly, one of the most interesting and important of these 'niceties' is the tension between the 'enabling' aims of social work practice and the 'constraining' effects of social work language. The central argument of this book is that the language which social workers are trained to use in order to free clients very often has the effect of imprisoning them anew.

In the chapters that follow we develop this argument in detail. At this point in our discussion we want to state in fairly blunt terms how we think our position differs from other general approaches in the field. We begin with 'traditional social work'. By this term we mean casework, systems models, the unitary approach, task-centred work, group work, and crisis intervention. We accept that these approaches differ in many important respects. Nevertheless, in our view, what unites all is the aim of bringing about the adjustment of the client to presently existing conditions in society. Traditional social work is therefore about the technical management of personal problems and the maintenance of order. Language here is described in neutral terms. It is seen as a mere tool of communication which social workers use to communicate with co-workers and clients. We object to this because it gives a one-sided view of social work language. Only the enabling side of language is expressed. Its limiting aspects are ignored.

The main front opposition to traditional social work is radical

1

social work. The collective term is problematic since it includes many conflicting strands of social work theory and practice, e.g. labelling theory, critical psychoanalytical models, Marxism, feminism, and discourse theory. It is difficult to claim successfully that these strands add up to a coherent and united alternative to traditional social work. Yet they do have at least two general features in common. They criticise traditional social work on the grounds that it (a) applies an ahistorical view of social work values, and (b) neglects to itemise the structural context in which personal problems are produced and reproduced. Our book uses Marxist and feminist forms of social work as examples of the radical turn taken by social work since the 1960s. On occasions in our discussion we will make strong objections to many aspects of radical theory and practice. Like Sedgwick (1982: 237) we hold the view that 'the politicisation of [social work] problems by radicals and left wingers is, very often of considerable crudity. The [client] tends to be slotted into the general case offered by a certain radical ideology, at the expense of the specifics.' At the same time, we want to defend ourselves from the simple-minded judgement that those who are critical of radical positions must, by that fact, be for traditional forms of theory and practice. Constructive criticism is a valid third option and we have sought to exploit and develop it in the pages of this book.

A dialectical and realist view

We argue for a dialectical and realist view of social work. Since much of this book is spent attacking others for lack of clarity and precision in their use of language, we ought to try to be clear and precise about what we mean by these two keywords. By *dialectical* we mean a view of social work which recognises that all things exist in time; and, because of this, they are contradictory, transient, and changeable. We use the term *realism* to refer to the view that a real, objective world exists independently of consciousness, which is, however, ascertainable by consciousness. We include nature, history, and society in our notion of the real world. Our argument is that the conduct of individuals cannot be understood accurately unless it is placed in the context of natural, historical, and social relations.

It will be said against us that many of the beliefs and attitudes that we call 'realist' are already standard features of traditional social work. For example, few adherents of casework, the unitary approach, task-centred work, group work, or crisis intervention would dissent from the proposition that the conduct of individuals is influenced by natural, historical, and social factors. We do not doubt that this is the case. The difficulty is that implicitly, and sometimes in very explicit ways they suggest that the 'normal' relationship between the individual and society is one of harmony. From this it follows that the task of social work is to restore harmony if, for some 'abnormal' reason, it is disrupted. For example, Douglas (1979: 16) attests that 'the restoration of *functional normality* is the basis of social work practice' (our emphasis).

Radical social workers also want to act. But they reject the idea that a natural state of 'functional harmony' exists between individuals and society. Rather they submit that individuals are divided by relations of class, gender, and race and by other types of power. Conflict is seen as the inevitable response to unequal and oppressive social conditions. It will be noted that realist assumptions are very much to the fore in the radical perspective. Individuals are seen as shaped, constrained, and sometimes crushed and destroyed, by social and historical conditions over which they have little control. Unlike traditional social workers, radicals argue that the way to change individuals and alleviate personal suffering is to transform the unequal and oppressive conditions which disfigure social relations. Social workers are called upon to play an instrumental role in raising the clients' consciousness and harnessing the clients' own experience as the main resource in undermining class domination, patriarchy, racial stereotyping, etc.

The routine objection to realist theory is that it produces an overdeterministic model of human behaviour. Social action is 'explained' as the reflection of real forces in the real world. Any notion that the individual is a skilled, knowledgeable, and creative actor in social life is set to one side. Instead, realist theory is accused of endorsing a passive view of human relations: the individual is portrayed as a mere artery through which the power of the social system flows.

This objection certainly applies to both traditional and radical versions of realism in social work. Thus the 'helping' role of traditional social work often involves the citizen in examining the validity of his or her feelings about his or her 'problem'. In particular, angry and negative feelings are seen as dangerous abnormalities that threaten the social order. The notion that these feelings represent accurate and meaningful condemnations of deadening social relations is never seriously developed. Instead social work intervention amounts to a powerful and systematic attempt to persuade the client to adjust to 'the real world', i.e. to society as it currently exists. For its part, radical social work argues that social problems are determined. When a child is beaten to death in the family, when a household falls into chronic debt, when people develop addictions for alcohol or drugs, it happens for real, objective reasons. This position, and the dilemmas it raises about human freedom and creativity, have been quite sufficient to deter many people from calling themselves 'radicals' or 'realists'. Certainly, many social workers feel uncomfortable with an approach which seems to argue that freedom is illusory and that personal conduct is structurally determined.

However, there is no reason why realism should be fated to produce conservative and fatalistic conclusions about the nature of human behaviour. Furthermore, there is no logical reason why the proposition that our subjective thoughts, feelings, and actions are objectively structured should lead to the denial of freedom. For example, it would be absurd to argue that knowledge of the objective factors which cause a family to suffer a gas or electricity disconnection cannot be used by social workers to act upon these conditions to modify them. Equally, it would be excessive to maintain that the knowledge that a social worker gains through working with delinquents or drug users is of no value in developing our understanding of the objective causes of delinquency or drug abuse. The basic point is well expressed by Sayers in his interesting and important defence of realist philosophy:

> In so far as we come to understand the causes and principles governing the operation of things, and learn to use this knowledge, to that extent we are no longer the mere passive victims of our conditions. We then have the capability of being active and free with respect to them.
>
> (Sayers 1985: 206)

This is the position that we shall exploit in the following pages.

Realism is but one side of our approach. The need to establish a dialectical view of social work is of equal importance in our scheme of things. We hold that our thoughts, feelings, and actions are not static or inflexible. The same must be said of the natural, historical, and social context in which these thoughts, feelings, and actions occur. Social life is dynamic and contradictory. Social problems and social requirements can never be fully foreseen or planned. The attitude which social workers adopt to established theoretical outlooks and methods of intervention must be not merely critical, but also self-critical. This is what dialectical thought means.

Yet so much exists in institutionalised social work to deter attitudes of thought which are consistently dialectical. Before an individual can become a qualified and employable social worker it is necessary to pass through certain rules of accreditation. In order to 'belong' to the occupation, one must learn recognised occupational skills, knowledge, and the official language. The communication of authority and competence depends upon the efficient use of skills, knowledge, and language. However, the relationship between the social workers' perception of outward competence and their internal attitude towards it is very complex. Often, social workers may know what to do or say in order to give the external appearance of competence, but inwardly harbour feelings of self-doubt and confusion. Society requires social workers to do the right thing, even in circumstances where they do not know what the right thing is, and where several courses of action are seen as equally right. It follows that social workers labour under strong institutional pressures to camouflage and repress uncertainty and, instead, to appear decisive. This may be manifested in the social workers' relationship with co-workers and line management, but it becomes especially intense in their relations with clients and representatives of external professional groups who liaise with them regularly and are therefore in a position to form an opinion on the competence of their professional practice, e.g. judges, doctors, the police, and the media. Expressed sociologically, in these situations the normative framework produces rigid and inflexible actions and responses in the social worker which deny doubt and contradiction. In this way, social work can very easily fall from being an activity which seeks to help clients and alleviate distress, into being an activity which responds to questions of client need, care, and the nature of the social work task with mechanical stereotypes.

Received ideas and social work

Every profession develops a professional language. 'The
language employed', writes Edelman (1977:60) 'implies that
the professional has ways to ascertain who are dangerous,
sick or inadequate; that he or she knows how to render them
harmless, rehabilitate them or both; and that the procedures
for diagnosis and treatment are too specialised for the lay
public to understand or judge them.'

The professional language of social work is made up of the received
professional wisdom. It constitutes the immediate and concrete
context in which entrants to the profession are socialised and
practise. The language is a form of power. It orders the
professional world and is the main vehicle for communicating
competence externally.

Traditional social work is composed of a set of key received
ideas relating to professional values and standards of practice.
For example, in the USA, the National Association of Social
Workers (NASW 1958) listed as basic values of social work,
respect for 'individual uniqueness', the right to 'the realization of
the full potential of each individual', and tolerance of 'the
differences that exist between individuals'. In Britain, the British
Association of Social Workers (BASW 1975) has drawn up a
similar list. The British 'code of ethics' calls upon social workers
to apply principles of 'self-determination', 'non-judgementalism',
'compassion', 'professional responsibility', and 'confidentiality'.
Still more recently in Britain, the Barclay Report (1982: 145), on
the future of social work, affirmed that professional social workers
agree that all persons have a need for 'respect', 'understanding',
'justice', and 'equality'. The received ideas of professional social
work must be translated into action. Each value comes with an
approved code of intervention which defines practice methods
and goals. For example, Hollis (1969: 15) writes that to achieve
the professional value of 'self-determination' the caseworker
should be 'supportive', 'open', and 'accepting', and use specialised
techniques to develop the clients' own reasoning capacities.
Consciousness of this is part of the received tradition and ethos
of casework.

Not every social worker is a caseworker. Within traditional
social work important subcultural variations exist. Different
subcultures negotiate and exchange received ideas and codes of

intervention in different ways. For example, a variety of therapeutic methods to bring 'care' and 'concern' into the social work relationship have been devised. These methods include psycho-social techniques of interaction associated with casework, forms of situational analysis used by group workers, and the verbal or written work agreements favoured in contract and task-centred work.

If it is true that not every social worker is a caseworker, it is equally true that not every social worker is a traditional worker. As we have already noted, radical social work has made significant inroads into social work theory and practice. Radical social workers are extremely critical of traditional received ideas and codes of intervention. For example, from the perspective of Marxist social work, 'care' and 'concern' are the buzz words of an occupation which historically has fulfilled the role of satisfying capital's demand for a compliant, healthy work-force. Traditional received ideas are explained away as examples of class ideology. They function to mystify the public with the illusion that capitalism really does care for the needy and the poor. Nowhere is the real purpose of the traditional language exposed more nakedly than in the demands of traditionalists to 'keep politics out of the personal'. For Marxists, the point is precisely that class politics define the 'personal' from the outset. Marxist commentaries have been recognised as a necessary reaction to the gaps in traditional social work. However, the received ideas of Marxist radical theory and practice contain many insufficiencies and the work of feminist social workers has been particularly important in exposing them. Feminists have attacked Marxists for making extravagant claims about the importance of class in social work relations while at the same time neglecting the family, gender and sexuality. As a result, the whole question of male power and the subordination of women has been side-railed.

At this point in our discussion we do not propose to give too much detail on received ideas and codes of intervention in traditional, Marxist, and feminist social work. After all, this subject occupies us for the whole of the first three chapters of the book. We do not want this introduction to pre-empt our discussion there. However, at the very least we hope that we have done enough to impress three major points upon the reader. In the first place, the language which social workers use is not neutral. It is evocative of a historically specific set of professional received ideas and codes of intervention which organise the professional world. What Wittgenstein (1969: 229) said of the communication of certainty can also be said of the language of social work: 'our talk gets its meaning from the rest of our proceedings.' Secondly, the received ideas of social work consist of key terms such as 'respect', 'at risk', 'tolerance', 'in need of care', 'confidentiality', 'professional responsibility', etc., which have high elasticity and resist close definition. As Cohen observes:

> They are symbols which condense, rearrange and mix-up beliefs, speculations, perceptions, verified facts, expectations, memories and emotions. Most of the terms used by the helping professions combine a high degree of unreliability (in their diagnosis, prognosis and prescription of the right treatment), with an ambiguous set of constraints upon clients.
>
> (Cohen 1985: 175)

Thirdly, the professional language of social work is a form of power. It enables the social worker to label the client and regulate behaviour which is defined as 'abnormal', 'inadequate', 'unhealthy', or 'at risk'.

We will pursue the third point at length in Chapter 4 which is devoted to an investigation of discourse theory and social work. Discourse theory is not yet widely used in social work training or practice. However, in our own work with students, co-workers, and clients we have found it useful to explore social work relations through the prism of discourse theory. Let us say a little about what is involved. Discourse theory examines the language, knowledge, myths, and assumptions that underpin a particular manifest position. The collective term for language, knowledge, assumption, and myth is *discourse*. Discourse theory argues that specific discourses can be shown to produce problems and impose solutions on the individual. For example, consider the therapeutic discourses that have grown up around investigations into the needs of 'man'. They have laid down minimal requirements and standard criteria to identify and measure human satisfaction and well-being. If these requirements are absent 'man' is said to be unwell and this 'condition' is made the target of 'problem-solving' strategies and manoeuvres. Social problems are said to be 'produced' and solutions 'imposed' upon 'man' by discourse because these strategies and manoeuvres spring from the nature of the discourse rather than the felt needs of 'man'. It is as if discourse sets out a standard identikit picture of human needs and requires every individual to comply with it, including those individuals who feel no positive connection with the picture whatsoever.

In our experience, discourse theory is a relevant and useful approach for understanding many aspects of social work in the present day. Consider the example of contract work. A routine criticism that contract workers make of traditional social work is that it contains 'hierarchical' and 'anxiety-making' tendencies which shut out the client. The client is said to feel uncertain of the aims of practice, suspicious of social work protocol, and unreceptive to the task of taking active initiatives on problem-solving and goal-setting. The contract approach seeks to counteract all of this. It aims to use work contracts as mechanisms for building genuine partnerships with clients. Among the positives regularly claimed for contract work are higher levels of openness, honesty, power-sharing, and mutuality in social work. On this occasion we want to focus on mutuality. The claim of mutuality is associated, above all, with the work of Maluccio and Marlow (1974). They argue that mutuality brings greater equality and sensitivity to the social work relationship. What is the basis for this claim? Logically, it has no basis in experience for it is precisely the absence of mutuality in everyday social work that the authors are commenting upon. If the idea of mutuality does not come from experience where does it come from? It can only come from ideas. That is, we can infer what Maluccio and Marlow mean by mutuality because we know what 'lack of trust', 'anxiety', 'coercion', 'manipulation', etc., mean in social work. To put the point in the terminology of discourse theory: we have an inkling of what mutuality *signifies* (means) because we are aware of how it differs from other *signs* (social work ideas) in the *signifying system* (language of social work) (for further details see Rojek and Collins 1987).

Discourse theory shows very clearly that our capacities to communicate and understand what is going on are not simply products of personal will. Language may not put words into our mouths, but it does put us in positions of authority and subordination in relation to one another. For example, Spender (1980) and other feminist writers have shown how the language of patriarchy situates men as reasonable, business-like, active, and decisive, and presents women as passive, maternal, submissive, docile, and virtuous. A similar ordering of power is accomplished by social work language in its placing of workers and clients and its identification of rights and duties, needs and desires. We shall examine this process in detail in the chapters that follow.

Received ideas and ideology

At first sight the concept of received ideas may seem to be identical to the concept of ideology. The latter has been widely discussed in social work. Two levels of ideology are usually distinguished. At the general level, social workers are said to work in a society which is permeated by the dominant class ideology and patriarchy. That is, our everyday thoughts, feelings, and actions are described as shaped by underlying relations of power. Social work is required to cut through the distortions, illusions, and false assumptions of ideology (see Pritchard and Taylor 1978; Corrigan and Leonard 1978; Bolger *et al.* 1981; Jones 1983). At the specific level, social workers are said to be in the service of the professional 'practice' ideology. The concept of practice ideology refers to 'those ideas, beliefs, theories, etc., which inform the professionals' day-to-day work' (Clark with Asquith 1985: 103). Practice ideology may be at odds with the dominant ideology in society. In some cases, it may even be defined in opposition to the dominant ideology. Marxist and feminist forms of social work are good examples of this. Practice ideology in social work is the main basis for communicating competence externally (see Rees 1978; Smith 1980).

Our discussion of received ideas and codes of intervention in professional social work differs from the concept of 'practice ideology' in at least two major respects. In the first place, the concept of practice ideology tends to emphasize the constraining and limiting effects of professional ideas and language. Thus, Leonard (1984: 188) comments that social workers utilize 'definitions of the situation of the marginal by powerful others who are not marginal'. Traditional social work, in particular, is criticised for being prescriptive rather than analytical and authoritarian rather than authoritative in its treatment of social problems. In contrast, the concept of received ideas lays stress on the dual effect of professional ideas and language. Received ideas and protocols are seen as both enabling and constraining.

The second respect in which the concept of received ideas differs

10

is this. The concept of practice ideology suggests a unified ideology which is imposed in uniform fashion upon members of the profession. Our analysis of how social workers are trained and how they relate to clients, co-workers, and line management does not reinforce the practice ideology position. Instead of unity we have encountered division, and instead of the uniform imposition of received ideas and language we have found unevenness and reaction. By using the term *received idea*, we aim to emphasise that what is given in social work training and practice is not always accepted. The received context of thought, ethical values, and practice is not a subject for blind submission among social workers, but an arena for struggle and dissent.

Received language and felt need

Although our style of argument aims to be analytical and detached, the origins of this book are emotional. We want to see efficient social services in a caring society. Like many other people, we are frustrated by the inadequate funding of social work departments, the bureaucracy of local authority procedures, and the low levels of public understanding as to what social workers actually do. Yet in all conscience, we feel unable to put all the blame on the shoulders of the government, county, and town-hall bureaucrats and a credulous public. Some of the blame lies with social workers themselves. There are major defects in the system of training, the organisation of practice, and the career structure. These defects are often most palpable in the language of social work because it is through this language that values are affirmed or ignored and meaningful contact is made between the social worker and clients, co-workers, line managers, and other representatives of the helping professions.

When we listened to social workers talking about the need to give clients 'self-respect', 'support', 'a decent life', we felt curiously motivated. While we were strongly drawn to these words, we could not help but observe how ambiguous, contentious, imprecise, and elusive they were. What is more, without any firm means of evaluation, the words degenerated into empty slogans which, in the final analysis, help no one and accomplish nothing. The received language of social work, and we mean this to apply to both traditional and radical social work, seemed wide of the mark of our felt needs. Such a condition carries with it obvious dangers:

Language which has ceased to express felt needs is empty
rhetoric. Much of the language carries a heavy legacy of
past attachments and commitments: it is always an open
question whether we genuinely share these commitments or
are simply mouthing the platitudes which are their sign.

(Ignatieff 1984: 138)

Such, we believe, is the condition of much writing and talking
about need and care in modern social work. The words are
ceremoniously presented at conferences and inserted in press
releases. However, they are far harder to pin-point in practice.
Where there is a gap between avowal and experience, the language
fails to carry conviction. It becomes a token, a mere sign of tribal
membership. To paraphrase Adorno (1973: 20), social workers
'wear it in their buttonholes'.

There are obvious historical reasons for this state of affairs in
social work. Historically speaking, social work has been deeply
influenced by humanism, i.e. the philosophy that 'man' is
composed of common, natural capacities, needs, and wants which
can be developed progressively by sober, rational guidance. The
received ideas and language of social work, in its traditional and
radical versions, make extensive use of humanist concepts. The
language is bolstered by constant reference to 'belonging',. 'shared
need', 'commitment', 'positive feelings', 'negative feelings',
'necessary actions', etc. Moreover, the language places the social
worker at the centre of the social problem and requires him or
her to act. This is particularly evident in traditional social work
which often portrays the social worker in a heroic role, struggling
to alleviate suffering and distress in others. Thus, Pincus and
Minahan (1973: 43) characterise social workers as 'change agents'
with a 'faith in a rational approach to problem-solving'. It is very
important to add that it is not only traditional social work that
places the social worker at the centre of things. Radical social
work, notably in its Marxist and feminist forms, regularly
describes the social worker as a catalyst who raises the repressed
or distorted consciousness of the client and takes action.

The active role of the social worker is taken for granted in the
received thought and language of social work. Yet it does not
automatically follow that it is justified. Let us be more specific.
In acting, social workers make assumptions about their needs
and make judgements about the needs of others. However, when
an objective basis for these assumptions and judgements is called

for, social workers often run into difficulties. Social workers cannot always be sure that a child needs to be removed from its family; they cannot be certain that the family or the class system actually engenders the effects which they attribute to it. Yet society requires them to be forever certain. Moreover, the professional bodies and training agencies reinforce the requirements for decisiveness.

To be decisive is one thing, to be accurate is another. The received language places so much emphasis on professional decisiveness that accuracy tends to be left behind. For example, traditional social workers are encouraged to nourish sentiments of 'community belonging' in the client. Yet this seems inaccurate and ineffective in a market society which fuels private competition, self-interest, and possessive individualism to such a degree that the question of community is turned into an abstraction. Similarly, even radical social workers speak a dead language when they urge class action among their clients under social conditions in which class organisation (let alone class action) is objectively denied. The majority of people in our society define themselves by how they differ from others rather than how they resemble them. They regard life as fragmentary, discontinuous, unstable, and subject to violent change. A market collapses, a cash limit holds, and they are out of work. Criminal violence, nuclear weapons, lightning strikes, cancers, and infections seem to surround them in a bewildering chain of impersonal and uncontrollable threats. Under such conditions, when the everyday life of so many people is obviously and demonstrably experienced as uncertain and hazardous, the language of common needs and collective responses is apt to seem remote and superficial.

Received ideas: chapter by chapter

We shall refer to the gap between language and meaning, representation and action, as the *cultural crisis* of modern social work. In our view, it is as important as the problem of inadequate funding, but it has received much less attention. Our book should be read as a contribution to raising the profile of this matter with social work educators, students, managers, and rank-and-file personnel. The book is divided into five chapters.

In Chapter 1 we explore received ideas and jargon in traditional social work. We comment on the origins of traditional social work and the present-day use of traditional language. Our discussion uses examples from psychoanalytical terminology, core values, and the communication process in a Probation After-Care Agency to illustrate the ambiguity and elusiveness of traditional received ideas.

Chapter 2 examines the Marxist alternative in social work. Marxists claim to transcend the dilemmas of traditional theory and practice to produce a more accurate, effective, and reliable form of social work. We assess the validity of this claim, and argue that the pursuit of accuracy, effectiveness, and reliability has led to important divisions in Marxist theory and practice. We examine the nature of these divisions and argue that each perpetuates received ideas on the nature of social work which are quite as restrictive as the traditional received ideas that they are designed to replace.

The theme of internal division continues in Chapter 3. Here we examine the question of women, social work, and feminism. Women played the major part in getting professional social work off the ground. Moreover, they predominate as both providers and recipients of welfare services today. Yet their economic and administrative power in social work bears no relation to their numerical strength. In this chapter, we explore the reasons for this, using historical and social policy data to build our case. We argue that feminist writers have produced a luminous critique of the received ideas and codes of intervention in traditional social work. Furthermore, their analysis of social work exposes the pitfalls of approaches which rely too heavily on assumptions of class struggle. Nevertheless, feminists have fallen into serious disagreements along the way. Some of the most significant relate to the role and prospects of feminist action through social work in patriarchal society. Our discussion examines the nature of these disagreements and attempts to assess their implications.

Chapter 4 addresses the question of the humanist influence in social work. We use ideas drawn from discourse theory to expose some of the limitations of humanist social work. In the course of the chapter we make rather lengthy forays into the theoretical writings of a number of discourse theorists, notably Lacan and Foucault. We make no apology for doing so. Discourse theory may well be unfamiliar to many of our readers. Certainly, there have been less than a handful of attempts to apply it in the field of social work. Therefore our discussion is designed in part as an introduction to this complicated, difficult, but ultimately rewarding approach. In addition we seek to show clearly that the assumptions of discourse theory have important and far-reaching implications for social work. If its assumptions are correct, both traditional and radical social work are shaken to their foundations.

Chapter 5 closes the book. Here we dwell on the unusual nature of social work relations in modern society. Whereas social life is dominated by strong pressures to repress strong emotions and disguise anxiety, social work relations aim to confront strong emotions and anxieties frankly and in an atmosphere which is relaxed and non-judgemental. The desire to help with intimate problems carries with it risks. Our discussion examines how helpers and carers can become the victims of violent acts from the recipients of help and care. We also explore the potential of community-orientated social work in modern society. The chapter ends by branching out into a discussion of the nature of society in which modern social work is conducted. We maintain that the received ideas and language of social work are rooted in a society which no longer exists. Bourgeois society was founded upon the assumptions that social life is orderly and bound by unbreakable laws of emotion; that social inequality reflects natural justice; and that language is a mere tool of communication which can be used to produce fixed and definite meanings. The conditions of modernism, the conditions of modern social life, are very different. Modernism shows the world to be many-sided and relativistic; it argues that nothing is certain and that all organisations and associations are provisional; moreover, it nourishes an extremely sceptical view of the possibility of fixed and definite meaning. Many of the most urgent and serious problems that modern social workers encounter arise from the mismatch between the 'heavy legacy' of received ideas and the nature of modern society.

Social work is about words. It is also about people. Although words and the meaning of words are ineluctably at the heart of our considerations, it would be superficial to regard our book as merely a study of social work language. It is a study of *power*. When we ask what the language of social work is, we also ask what it is in our culture to be 'social', and what forms of social action are officially sanctioned, repressed, and punished. We ask what normality is, and how normative moral criteria in our culture are defined, consecrated, and passed on through the generations. In short, we pose the question of what 'civilized' society finds intolerable.

1

Received ideas and jargon
in traditional social work

Despite the growth of social work literature in the post-war period, especially in the late 1960s and 1970s, only a small amount has been written on the topic of language and received ideas. Talk and talking have been seen as the stock in trade of social work. However, in the late 1970s and 1980s the focus has moved on to the developing micro/macro debate and the whole question of politics and social work. It is interesting that this has occurred without social work having established a precise position on its traditional received ideas and language: that of therapy and individual help. Biestek, in his classic text on casework, seems to suggest that the whole business of language and ideas is peripheral to the real world of social work. 'No exploration or definition can do justice to a living thing: words have a certain coldness, while relationships have a delightful warmth' (Biestek 1961: viii). From this standpoint, social work appears to be above mere ideas and is unfettered by language. Yet, at the same time, this ignores the fact that some of the most common received ideas in social work such as 'respect', 'individualisation', and 'self-determination' are generalised global terms, placed against a backcloth of 'democracy' and 'Christianity' which in turn is vast in its generality and totality. Problems about the definition of 'democracy' and 'Christianity' have rarely been addressed in the social work literature. Instead it has been assumed that the meaning of these concepts is something that we hold in common as core cultural values. As such, their meaning is said to be as obvious and self-evident as what it is to be British or American. Such assumptions betray what Younghusband (1973) calls 'an innocent arrogance', for it is certain that some people in western societies reject Christian and democratic values. Moreover, even among those who hold fast to them, there are important disagreements as to what they actually mean.

In this chapter we argue that social workers talk to one another, and write for one another, as if the content of their talk and writing were self-explanatory. So accustomed are they to dealing in the institutionalised received ideas and jargon of social work that no explanation seems necessary either for themselves or for others. We contend that this assumption is seriously mistaken. The received thought and language of traditional social work is often vague, imprecise, and self-contradictory. Later we shall consider examples from the present day. Before that we want to show that vagueness, imprecisions, and self-contradiction are nothing new. On the contrary, they have been evident since the first stirrings of organised social work in the west.

A brief historical perspective

It is not our intention to present a detailed historical perspective. This task has been more than adequately covered elsewhere (see Stedman-Jones 1971; Parry *et al.* 1979; Jones 1983). Rather our intention is to highlight in a succinct and disciplined manner some of the basic ambiguities that have beset social work language from the earliest days. Historically speaking, social work has struggled in its development between perceptions of its task as friendship and art or as profession and science. The earliest social workers, like Octavia Hill, wrote of social work as little more than a form of patronage. 'District visiting', she wrote in 1893, 'was less work than neighbourly kindliness taking its natural course in the flow of help to individuals who had long been known' (cited in Timms 1968: 76). For his part, Bernard Bosanquet, writing in 1901, emphasised the importance of personality in social work practice:

> Social work is thought of as something spontaneous, human, sociable; an effort to gain direct contact with the human nature of those around us. In it we devote to others not our peculiar acquired skill, but ourselves, our heart and soul.
>
> (Cited in Timms 1968: 77)

There is a hint of moral crusade in these words and a glimmer of *noblesse oblige*. However, even in 1906 the literature of the Charity

Organisation Society (COS) provides evidence of moves to transform social work from a part-time activity of the rich and well-born into a skilled and professional activity which bore comparison with medicine: 'Doctors have to be educated methodically, registered and certificated. Charity is the work of the social physician. It is to the interests of the community that it should not be entrusted to novices or to dilettanti or to quacks' (Loch 1906: xix).

At the same time the role of rigorous systematised professional education in social work was being emphasised: 'The impulse to do good, may if untainted, lead straight to evil doing ... the good heart unschooled by the good head will probably fall into dangerous paths – in a word ... training is an essential for social service' (Urwick 1904: 180).

'The good heart', 'the good head', 'dangerous paths' – these are the hale metaphors of a rising professional class strong in their conviction of the worth of their enterprise. There is much good cheer about these ideas. Who can doubt that a 'good heart' and a 'good head' are desirable qualities for the social worker? Yet when it comes to trying to define these terms, or to provide guidelines for their cultivation, all is obscure, coy, questionable, and ambiguous. Nevertheless, this is the typical style of thought and language which in 1903 launched the COS School of Sociology – the beginnings of formal social work education in Britain and its twin thrusts of professionalism and training.

The COS School set up a vital divide which was to have far-reaching effects on the development of British social work. The divide was between the approved, trained workers who passed through the COS system of education successfully, and the uninitiated, untrained men and women who were now to stand outside the professional body. At the same time, social work writers became increasingly concerned with enhancing the status of social work by developing a 'scientific' professional language. Similar and interesting comparisons have been made with the development of medical dominance in the mental health field in the USA and the growth of positivist approaches in psychiatry (Kovel 1981). The following passage represents the new attitude of mind:

> The terms in which truths are expressed often belong to a
> past age; have we not all been at times uneasily conscious
> that the mere appeal to fundamental principles like self help,

independence, thrift and the like, has lost much of its force, and that these principles must be recast, brought into new connections with current ways of thinking, *clothed in a new language?* For it is unquestionably true that the new generation is receptive enough, but as always demands a new preparation of its food.

(Urwick 1904: 182; emphasis ours)

Unfortunately as Yelloly (1980) has observed, for the first forty years of the twentieth century, social work in Britain produced no literary giants to provide 'a new preparation of its food' or to comprehensively influence the development of social work education.

This was something of a contrast to the situation in the USA. In 1917 the publication *Social Diagnosis* by Mary Richmond had been seen as the first of a major series of conceptual accounts of the social work process and a basic textbook for American as well as British social workers. Although an attempt was made to address both environmental and psychological aspects of social work there was a predominant examination of the latter. Basic steps in the helping process were described in the language of medicine – study, diagnosis, and treatment. The language was to influence the thinking of Felix Biestek and Florence Hollis over forty years later and much of the ideas and thinking of social workers in the present day. At the heart of this thinking was the idea of the defective or diseased organism to which some sort of therapeutic intervention could be applied. In the USA this model received powerful reinforcement from the strong development of psychiatric social work whose practitioners worked closely with medical personnel and were therefore influenced by medical ways of thought and clinical approaches to practice.

The incorporation of psychoanalytic terminology

In general this movement towards psychiatric thinking was further confirmed by the rapid assimilation of psychoanalytic ideas by the leading American social workers in the 1920s and 1930s. Yelloly (1980) and Timms (1983) have given detailed accounts of the development of the Diagnostic and Functionalist schools in the United States during that period. We shall concentrate here on the contribution of the Diagnostic school of British social work.

We do not say that the Diagnostic school was the only influence upon the professional development of social work in Britain. Indeed, its influence may have been somewhat restricted and partial. But we do submit that this restricted and partial influence was of great significance. Nowhere was this clearer than in the diagnostic language which began to trip easily from the tongues of many leading British social work educators. This language revealed the deep influence of psychoanalytic thought with a focus on the relationship of the individual to the external world and the ego's reactions to the drives of the id and the demands of the super-ego. Psychoanalytic ideas were seen as the only effective method of altering personality structure; and insight at that time was seen as a primary goal and major strategy of intervention. It is interesting to consider the influence of leading exponents of the Diagnostic School such as Annette Garrett, Charlotte Towle, Lucille Austin and Florence Hollis upon British social work in the 1950s, 1960s, and 1970s. Agency records often revealed generalised and vague phrases such as 'I shall support and build up this client's ego strengths'; or 'I shall attempt to help Mrs B gain insight into her problems which are revealed in outbursts of aggression towards her husband.' Words like 'ego strengths', 'insight', 'acting out', 'resistant', 'manipulative', 'interpretation', 'testing out', 'transference', and 'overidentify' began to percolate into the language of the British social work scene. During the early post-war years psychoanalytic ideas borrowed from American sources became received wisdom in the thinking of leading British social work educators. What is interesting is that these crucial ideas were rarely clearly defined. Understanding them was a matter of feeling and sensitivity, the 'good heart' and 'the good head', rather than precise enquiry. Often confused social work educators passed on their own diluted ideas to bewildered workers and students. Geoffrey Parkinson commented in a trenchant and pungent manner of these developments:

> Many of the noted social work theorists of recent times have plagiarised their insights from the work of Freud and Melanie Klein and hoped we would match *our* methods to *their* ideas. Carmelite casework, its nods and grunts and germ-free insights, was offered to clients in mouldy little offices all over England.
>
> (Parkinson 1977: 221)

The most detailed and comprehensive attempts to link psychoanalytic thought to social work practice were made by ego psychologists. However, the works of Wasserman (1968), Wood (1971), and Nursten (1974) were only part of a deluge of social work literature in the 1960s and 1970s. The rising stars of crisis intervention, task-centred casework, family therapy, systems thinking, and community social work have each in turn overtaken psychoanalytical models which became progressively more 'old hat' as social work marched on into the 1970s and 1980s. Unfortunately the prevailing fashions and fads left the psychoanalytic approaches only partially assimilated and partially understood. To put this into the terminology of discourse analysis, the psychoanalytic discourse clashed with new discourses in the field of social work long before the underlying tensions and blank spots in psychoanalytic thinking had been worked out.

We want to illustrate these remarks by turning to some recent examples from the present-day language of social work. Again our aim is to provide an indication of the powerful hold of received ideas in the field and also to show the vagueness, imprecision, and self-contradiction which surround them. We make no claim to provide a complete survey of the terrain.

Transference and counter-transference

In the late 1960s and early 1970s it became a sin to 'overidentify' with clients. Workers would confess to their supervisors that they were concerned and anxious because they found a client with similar attitudes and values to themselves – they even liked their clients! Transference and counter-transference ideas were sometimes used by supervisors to explain away workers' problems in relating to a client. Indeed they were even used by students in discussion with other students. Consider the following example:

> BEN. I don't see the supervisor as an authority figure – that's why I never bother to explain why I'm not here.
> ANOTHER STUDENT. You do have a difficulty about authority. Are you on good terms with your Dad?
> (Deacon and Bartley 1975: 75)

However, such explorations and explanations required an enormous commitment of time and energy which few supervisors and workers could afford. The result was a diluted and inconsistent application of the concepts of transference and counter-transference. It is clear that there are only limited references which devote attention to such phenomena in social work literature published in Britain (see Irvine 1956; Garrett 1968). Even standard texts such as Hollis seemed unable to make more than vague references: 'The worker must be free of the hostile counter-transference reactions that are so easily aroused in clients', (Hollis 1972: 106). It may have been that some social work educators understood such terminology, but how many social work students and workers were able to make practical use of such language and ideas in their day-to-day work? The idea of transference might give one account of client behaviour, it might suggest why a client acts in particular ways, but without detailed and extensive discussion with a skilled supervisor how did it, or can it, enable the worker to relate more effectively to the client? Furthermore, there are dangers that the concept of transference can be used by the worker to avoid confronting real issues. Szasz puts the point well when he writes that transference could become

> a successful defensive measure to protect ... from too intensive affective and real life involvement. For the idea of transference implies denial and repudiation of ... experience qua experience; it its place is substituted the more manageable construct of a transference experience [so that the worker] ... convinced himself that the client does not have these feelings and dispositions towards him ... but someone else. Transference experiences are so easily and so often misused; they provide a ready-made opportunity for putting the client at arm's length.
>
> (Szasz 1963: 51)

The 'acting-out' dilemma

'Acting-out' was a term borrowed from psychoanalytically based literature which often referred to clients who were unable to control id drives, who possessed 'weak super-egos', and who were unable to internalise conflicts. Social workers were encouraged to see relationships with such clients as very long-term endeavours. Movement in the relationship would be only marginal with an inability to change the 'diseased core' (Pollak 1960; Turner 1976). Many clients who were seen by probation officers could be conveniently labelled 'acting out'. The term could be used to justify contacts with clients which would wander rather aimlessly for years and to legitimate the social workers' inability to influence the clients' behaviour. It could also provide automatic prescriptions for 'treatment' which might enable social workers to feel secure in their knowledge of the clients' behaviour and, by extension, of their own ability to assess and diagnose (Pollak 1960; Sterba 1976). This is a clear example of the way in which the positivism of traditional psychiatry influenced social work in subtle and often misunderstood ways. It is not argued that a term such as 'acting out' was comprehensively understood and actively used by most social workers in the 1960s and 1970s, but that even in its incompleteness such a term influenced workers in their thinking and action. It fact, even as recently as 1981 'acting out' was used in a questionnaire presented to probation officers in order to differentiate the ways in which they approached their clients (Day 1981). The acting-out dilemma therefore illustrates one of the most common and serious unintended consequences of received ideas: reification, i.e. turning the client into a thing with standard needs, and standard wants, and requiring a standard method of intervention.

The 'resistant' client

If 'acting out' was a useful base for explaining away some of the problems social workers experienced in helping difficult clients then an idea such as 'resistance' provided another avenue to justify lack of success, lack of movement, and perhaps the inability of workers to communicate effectively with clients. 'Resistant' clients could be conveniently blamed for their inability to participate in, and profit from, therapeutic endeavours. For example, Hollis warned social workers to be wise to the tricks of the client:

> Occasionally workers may realise that the client is deriving marked gratification from talking freely about himself and seems to be making no effort to use the interview to move towards any improvement in himself or his situation ... the reason for discouraging it [talking freely] can be explained directly to the client thus leading him into a discussion of his resistance.

(Hollis 1972: 105-6)

This conveniently deflects attention from possible defects in the relationship skills of the worker. The Impact Studies (Folkard 1974) and work by Fischer (1976), Mullen and Dumpson (1972), and Rees and Wallace (1982) have all highlighted the problems workers have experienced in translating traditional casework skills from theory into practice. 'Resistant' was, and is, a term for legitimating the inabilities of a worker to help and communicate effectively with clients who live in poverty, poor housing, or ill health. Indeed, social workers have used the term all too readily to dismiss the hostile or obstructive reactions of clients as mere wrong-headedness. As one worker put it, 'We weren't too worried if the clients didn't like it. The theorists had explained that quite easily as "resistance" ' (Parkinson 1977: 221). In these and other ways the clients' own feelings and impressions about their situations are dismissed as having secondary importance.

Social workers are certainly alive to the ambiguities of the idea of resistance. Indeed it has been suggested that non-professional helpers can develop more effective helping relationships than professionals precisely because they are likely to have no technical knowledge or hang-ups about the 'resistant' client. Here are the comments of one American social worker:

> I sometimes feel like an inhibiting influence when I go along to introduce a homemaker to a client. When I leave they break out into their own language and vernacular. Empathy rather than sympathy sometimes comes more naturally to the homemaker than the professional worker.
>
> (Gans 1968: 454)

It should be added that it is not argued that all social workers frequently ascribe clients' inability to participate in the helping process to resistance, rather that this kind of language has had a subtle and insidious effect on the thinking of social workers over the years. It is one of the devices which workers can use to justify or excuse their own professional inadequacies and to enable them to survive, maintain a *raison d'être,* and continue to function in a demanding and stressful setting (Satyamurti 1979).

The inheritance of interpretation

Interpretation is a further example of an imprecise, misunderstood, and ambiguous concept which has its roots in psychoanalytic thinking and has been incorporated into the language of social work. For many social workers in the 1960s and 1970s interpretation was seen as an appropriate action which was equated with 'deep' casework. Even social work students were encouraged in this enterprise by their fieldwork supervisors. Here are the comments of one supervisor, encouraging a student social worker to be more cautious in his interactions with the headmaster of a school: 'You're feeling very angry about the general situation and transferring it to your particular situation. You don't want to be there – you're dissatisfied with yourself. Maybe you're angry that Jill has a foothold in the school and you don't' (Deacon and Bartley 1975: 72).

The influential work of Hollis incorporated such thinking into her 'direct treatment' categories using terminology such as 'reflective discussion' of the 'person situation configuration' with a partial focus upon encouraging clients to discuss reflectively their feelings, attitudes, and beliefs which had previously been withheld, unverbalised, or not recognised as significant. Clients were thus encouraged to recognise subjective responses and reactions which were considered unusual or inappropriate or which posed problems as a consequence. Similarly, Hollis suggested procedures for encouraging clients to think about the dynamics of their patterns of responses to situations. This involved the worker in encouraging clients to look at and study the relationship between different aspects of their behaviour in order to understand why they acted in certain ways. Yet another suggestion by Hollis was that workers should enable clients to reflectively consider the past and its effects on current functioning. Clients were to be helped to examine causative factors which, though they had occurred in the past, had become internalised to such a degree that they were part of their responses to current situations.

However, despite these grandiose-sounding techniques, several research studies which examine Hollis's classification system criticise her approach. In particular they note that workers spent very little time discussing internal conflicts and early experience, or offering interpretation to give clients insight into the causes of their present difficulties. Instead they tended to concentrate on the here and now and contented themselves with exploring and clarifying. In fact, several studies in the USA in the late 1960s revealed that only around 1-5 per cent of a worker's verbal interactions were concerned with early-life reflection and providing insight. So much for some of the sacred language of social work and those mystical words 'interpretation' and 'insight giving'.

'Testing out' the worker

Not surprisingly many clients are anxious and uncertain when they present themselves to social work agencies. There is a lot of evidence to suggest that many new clients are unclear about agency functions and the role of social workers (Rees 1978). Yet the early stages of contact have been stereotyped as a period when clients will test out workers to ascertain attitudes, assess limits, and evaluate boundaries to care and control. Such behaviour does not require a quasi-scientific explanation. A lack of clarity about agency function and the role of the social worker are legitimate bases for the feelings which clients experience. 'Testing out' implies a special mission. It suggests that the client is akin to a firebrand dedicated to usurping the social worker and overthrowing his or her influence. Surely this is unrealistic. Workers should be able to provide fairly clear, concise guidelines about their tasks and role and also about how this role can help the client. Recent literature has emphasised the importance of shared goals, contracts, and agreements (Reid 1978; Pincus and Minahan 1973). 'Testing out' unfairly implies tricks, games, devices, and subterfuge which surely denigrate the client who is striving to comprehend a new piece of interaction in a strange environment. In such instances, traditional social work rephrases, reinterprets, and readjusts reality to suit the perspective of the social worker. The client's perspective is often trivialised or dismissed in the process. Through the influence of received thought during social work courses and in agency offices, the internalisation of such concepts becomes uncritical. 'Testing out' becomes one more term in the battery of received ideas which is accepted on commonsense grounds and used by practicising social workers spontaneously and speedily, without much thought being given to its purpose or implications.

Manipulation and defence mechanisms

Manipulation is another term which has had a subtle, insidious influence on the social work process. It is far more ambiguous and vague than it seems at first sight. Clients who make requests for particular kinds of help have been sometimes rather too easily labelled as manipulative. The same might be said of clients who have expressed strong feelings and made critical comments to social workers. The desperation and depression of oppressed clients is more easy to manage if their hostile behaviour can be rationalised away. Satyamurti (1979) has written interestingly about this phenomenon. She argues that manipulation is one of the terms by which social workers maintain a distance from their clients and also adopt parent-like characteristics which enable them to deny or invalidate certain parts of clients' behaviour and status as citizens. Satyamurti quotes an apposite example of a female client who was well known locally as a useful source of information and help. She approached the social services department on account of problems with an electricity bill. At the team allocation meeting members thought this was an interesting opportunity to work with someone who was well known locally and had a fund of knowledge and experience of the area. However, the social worker involved found the ambiguity of the situation difficult and rejected the woman's claims to be considered as anything other than a client. 'She's so manipulative', Satyamurti (1979: 100) quotes him as saying, 'I can't stand her. She thinks she's better than the other clients but she's not.'

Some social workers and their managers find it difficult to perceive clients as people who can take on responsible roles and tasks (see, for example, Beresford and Croft 1986). The development of shared goals, contracts, and agreements mentioned earlier has encouraged social workers to see clients as 'partners' (Reid 1978; Pincus and Minahan 1973). Moreover, perceptions of clients as 'citizens' have suggested a narrowing down of the division between professional and client roles. However, when clients do take on more responsible, more powerful socially orientated tasks in order to obtain better social services or complain about an existing service, such as contacting the local paper, councillor, or MP, such behaviour is apt to be labelled as 'devious' or 'manipulative'. Once again we encounter an example of a received idea which is sometimes used by social workers to cope with client behaviour, to control it and deny its significance, enabling them to remove themselves from its immediate emotional impact. It is interesting that some of the most powerful pleas made on behalf of particular client groups have come from organisations unconnected with social workers, such as Claimants Unions, PROP, and many other self-help groups.

Similarly, the influence of Freudian-based thinking and language centred upon defence mechanisms has enabled social workers to cope more easily with their tasks. For example, Biestek

(1961: 72) has commented that part of the purpose of acceptance in social work is to 'help the client free himself from undesirable defences, so that he feels safe to reveal himself, to look at himself as he really is, and thus to deal with his problems and himself in a more realistic way'.

It is not claimed that social workers have a highly developed understanding of defence mechanisms, as only rarely have these been systematically incorporated into the social work literature (see Nursten 1974; Wood 1971; Wasserman 1968). Rather, our argument is that selective borrowings have occurred which have seeped through into field practice in a partial, fragmented manner. For example, social workers are reasonably familiar with terms such as 'denial', used when a client is thought to be unwilling to accept unpleasant stimuli coming either from inner drives or outer perceptions and literally refuses to consider that any problem exists or any negative, unpleasant event had occurred. The use of the term denial then places the worker in a position of superiority - and redefines the behaviour of the client.

It is also acknowledged that social workers are reasonably familiar with the concept of 'projection', whereby clients are seen to attribute their own unwanted impulses to an external object, either personal or non-personal, thus diverting bad feelings away from themselves. Once again, social workers use language to interpret, to redefine. They know the client is angry with himself or herself. Yet the client cannot express this and can only be angry with others. Thus language is used once again to explain away the behaviour of the client but no help of any other kind is given. Rather the worker is aware of what is happening within the client without being able to do much to change it or alleviate distress.

Deacon and Bartley provide an interesting fragment of a conversation between a student group and their supervisor :

FELIX: Ben didn't put up defences here because the group is very caring.

BEN: Not like the tutors.

SUPERVISOR: Ben is afraid of his own destructiveness.

BEN: Well, this seems to be the consensus. I suppose it might be something like that.

SUPERVISOR: You were afraid if you do let go you'd let go good and proper. You haven't realised that the others have enough defences to stand up to you.

(Deacon and Bartley 1975: 78)

Odd then that social workers seem less in touch with defence mechanisms such as rationalisation and intellectualisation. Rationalisation involves translating attitudes, beliefs, and behaviours into convincing form, despite evidence to the contrary! In this way they assume a ring of acceptability and individuals can thus provide logical reasons to themselves (and others) for behaviour which has been unconsciously influenced. At the same time, intellectualisation involves dealing with unacceptable, for example aggressive feelings by endless intellectual discussions about purposes and meanings. Perhaps intellectualisation and rationalisation are defence mechanisms often used by social workers themselves, as it is explicitly acknowledged that defence mechanisms are universal and necessary. However, denial and projection by clients are perhaps seen by social workers as more primitive mechanisms. They are labelled as the property of the immature – another word and idea which social workers are very fond of using to redefine the experience of their charges.

Conceptual annihilation and some alternatives

So often the client's reality is redefined into the social workers' terms. This redefinition has the purpose of insulating social workers from being threatened by the client's challenge to their 'real world'. This is but a small step from annihilation, which in its simpler form places the client at a point of marginality or insignificance – conceptual annihilation. In social work this crude form is rarely evident. But social work language does at times move towards a point where 'outsider' viewpoints are denied or liquidated. To enable this to be done outsider conceptions are translated into ideas compatible with the received thought and codes of one's own field of discourse. Several examples of this in social work have already been mentioned, 'manipulative', 'acting out', 'resistant', and 'transference' being particularly striking examples. By invoking these received ideas, social workers make the client's activity more consistent with their own discourse and are in danger of denying the client any existence outside that discourse. Robinson (1978: 2) has rightly emphasised the danger of the social worker 'being blocked from an adequate view of the clients' world and ... [being] able to impose his own definitions while ignoring or reinterpreting those of the client'.

Received ideas and codes can therefore be plugged into the client's problem to make it more intelligible to the social worker and also to enable the social worker to take some form of action. But the connection between the received thought and the clients' real problems or perception of their problems may be, to say the least, tangential. It might not be inappropriate for social workers to ponder the following passage:

> The challenge to [the social worker] who seeks to understand social reality, then is to understand the meaning that the actor's act has for him. If the observer applies only his own categories or theories concerning the meaning of acts he may never discover the meanings these same acts seem to have for the actors themselves. Nor can he discover how social reality is 'created' and how subsequent acts by human actors are performed in the context of *their* understandings.
>
> (Psathas 1972: 132)

Some core social work values

Psychoanalytically based thinking has also exerted considerable influence upon what have been defined as 'traditional' social work values (Plant 1970; CCETSW 1976; Timms 1983). While in recent years the 'traditional' value bases of social work have been expanded to include an increasing emphasis upon justice, equality, and the rights of clients it is nevertheless helpful to consider some of the 'traditional' values. We are thinking here of terms such as respect, individualisation, confidentiality, and self-determination. It is not our intention to examine these values in depth as they have been described elsewhere (Timms 1983; Clark with Asquith 1985); rather, we shall highlight some of the ambiguities contained within them. While it is sometimes argued that it is helpful for workers to be able to interpret core values on an *ad hoc* basis, at the same time they are used as a basis for legitimating decisions in debates with other professional groups associated with welfare, such as the press, police, teachers, health visitors, doctors, and lawyers. Furthermore, while it is intended that traditional social work values should lead to the utmost consideration of client need and to action on behalf of clients, on some occasions the reverse can be true and clients can become stereotyped, categorised, and objectified despite the best intentions of social workers to the contrary. By this we mean that social work like many other professions describes its basic concepts in technical terms, claims to have some consensus about what it is doing, and thus makes some attempt to classify its world: attempts which, in the long run, may not always be helpful to clients. We cannot readily talk about social work or practise social work without considering, examining, and understanding 'core' values. We agree with Timms (1983: 217) who suggests that social work should aspire to 'clarity and specificity' in its approach and that 'the problems of social work should not be left behind in 'the confident phrase and implicit contradictions'. However, as we have showed already in this chapter, and will show in more detail as the book continues, it is not easy for social workers to achieve clarity and specificity in practice or to avoid contradiction. Let us now begin our consideration of core values by taking the value of respect.

Respect

Biestek and Gehrig note that social work 'selects as its supreme value the innate dignity and value of the human person. It maintains that nothing in the world is more precious and noble than the person and that every person is worthy of respect' (cited in Timms 1983: 57). Now these intentions are clearly positive and commendable, and in their broad suggestions for the conduct of social workers they might be thought to be without reproach. Most significantly, encouragement is given to respect the unfortunate downtrodden outsiders who often remain at the bottom of the social pile. Such people often suffer from labelling which has negative connotations such as 'loony', 'nutter', 'down and out', 'alcky', and 'thief'. Respect suggests that social workers should cherish their outcast clients and work with them as means not ends. However, what also strikes us about respect is its breadth of meaning and its massive imprecision.

Respect is intended to have a specific meaning for social workers but as the earlier quote indicates it does exist at a high level of abstraction. It tends to focus on attitudes and feelings rather than considering the specific of action and interaction with others. Action and interaction are essential features of the social workers' day-to-day contacts with clients, colleagues, and other workers. It is these day-to-day contacts which provide the setting for the operationalising of respect. The role of the agency, the workers' obligation to the client, to the law, to their profession, and to their personal values all meet together in a complex state of tension and contradiction. Thus, respect becomes active, becomes alive in a complex set of interactions where other values impinge, and where the 'supreme value' of the person may well be subordinated to other considerations, e.g. lack of agency resources, other

32

priorities set by the agency, inadequate legislative provision, other calls upon the workers' time. To put it differently, respect for the person is submerged in a torrent of demands, which make it difficult to translate 'respect' into active practice. The intentions are praiseworthy. However, the reality may be somewhat different. Other considerations regularly militate against the sensitive and thoughtful operationalisation of respect.

Individualisation

Traditional casework theory, with its roots in Freudian personality theory, takes the individual – the single person – as the focus of intervention. Individualisation is indeed regarded as an essential value of social work. Students are taught to see clients as unique, special, and different. A client is also held to be unique in the actions he or she performs and plans to perform, actions which are dependent on language: 'Treatment is on an individual basis through the person to person relationship' (Biestek 1961: 25). Biestek also states that treatment is geared to promote the better adjustment of the client and is achieved by diagnosis of problems and goal-setting. There is a paradox here. Biestek says that social work is about relating to the client, 'individual case by individual case'. Yet the use of medical terms ('diagnosis', 'case', 'treatment') seems to point to standardised ideas and methods of intervention. They are, as we have seen before, ideas and methods which are likely to lead to reification, stereotyping, and thus a subtle, inexorable undervaluing of the client's individuality. Biestek himself seems to be conscious of the tensions in the concept of individuality. Although he speaks up for the sanctity of the individual, he also observes that the social worker should 'balance this emphasis with an awareness that human nature has some basic common characteristics and patterns' (Biestek 1961: 26). This recognition of 'common characteristics and patterns' also provides a loophole to prevent the worker from producing a unique meaningful relationship with the client. The worker can easily reduce the significance of an incident and explain whole series of incidents away by invoking some generalised, ideal-typical model of behaviour.

Individualisation should mean that the worker perceives and works with the client as both a unique and a special source of knowledge. Thus a more genuine interest is presented in the client as an actor, an agent who does things, and the social worker should provide a more honest appreciation of his or her identity as a person in the past, present, and future (Ragg 1976). It is our contention that individualisation has been so ill-defined and shot through with contradiction that many social workers have actually been confused and bemused by its implications. Many social workers have been distracted from the core meaning of individualisation by a variety of devices including professional socialisation and agency bureaucratisation. These will be discussed further at a later stage.

Self-determination

The same point can be considered from another angle by looking at the received idea of self-determination. Social workers have for long been conscious that the idea abounds in ambiguities (see McDermott 1975; Davies 1981; Timms 1983). Logically, self-determination implies a condition in which individuals are masters of their lives and have the power, freedom, choice, and knowledge to steer their future in whatever direction they elect to. Yet we have argued that the individual is, above all, a social creature. Individuals depend upon others for their emotional, physical, and economic well-being. They speak a language which is a social property, i.e. it existed before the individual was born, it shapes his or her perceptions and thinking, and it will continue to exist after the individual dies. There are then fairly insuperable barriers in the way of any view which sees the individual as consistently self-determining.

Instead of providing a clear, operational definition of self-determination, its exponents have tended to fudge the whole question. Thus,

> the right to freedom, to self-determination, is one of the most difficult of human values to comprehend. It contains so many variables that descriptions and definitions are precarious and hardly ever satisfying ... It appears an ever changing concept, affected by innumerable contemporaneous happenings in the culture of which it is found.
>
> (Biestek and Gehrig 1978: 4)

The temptation is strong to regard this statement as being so open-ended and wide ranging as to be almost meaningless. Items such as 'most difficult ... to comprehend', 'contains so many variables', 'an ever changing concept' leave one in no man's land. It is significant that this statement was made in 1978 at a stage when one might have expected sharper and more explicit definitions. Once again there is the suspicion that generations of social workers have completed their training and education with only a hazy comprehension of the meaning of a key received idea. Few studies have been made of the way in which the idea is actually used in practice. But Kossal and Kane in their small sample investigation note:

> great variability in the way practitioners interpret and apply the concept of self-determination in specific situations. The variability is even more striking because the sample was limited to one community ... and most respondents were graduates of a single school of social work ... respondents were able to justify very different courses of action as complying with self-determination.
>
> (Cited in Timms 1983: 20)

Thus the variability of the application of self-determination in practice is paralleled by the large differences in understanding of the concept. It may be that Biestek's original reservations about the limits of self-determination still hold true: 'The clients' right to self-determination ... is limited ... by the framework of civil and moral law and by the function of the agency' (Biestek 1961: 103).

There are other received ideas that we might have commented upon here, for example 'confidentiality'. But perhaps enough has been said to show that psychoanalytically based discourse in social work is influenced by a fairly narrow set of received ideas which constitute the ethos in which debate, practice, and innovation occur. Moreover, these ideas are far from being scientifically precise. On the contrary, as we have shown in example after example, they are vague, ambiguous, and fallible.

We have argued that psychoanalytic discourse has been a major historical influence on the development of social work in Britain and the United States. Few social workers have escaped unmarked. Even radicals have had, in a very deliberate and self-conscious way, to formulate their theories and practice alternatives in opposition to the traditional mould of casework discourse. None the less, we do not say that psychoanalytically based social work is the only discourse worth talking about or, for that matter, that it is only here that the ambiguities and paradoxes of received thought are evident. A full-scale study of received thought in many aspects of social work would, we believe, expose the received ideas and codes in rival areas of discourse, e.g. the unitary model, task-centred work, family therapy, etc. We have concentrated upon how received thought has influenced one aspect of present-day social work. We are not trying to provide an encyclopedia of its manifestations, causes, and consequences. However, in trying to clarify how received ideas and codes work, we do think that it is useful to go through one other example of social work discourse. The example refers to the in-house language of the social work agency. Eventually we will consider the Probation and After-Care Service, and draw on the work experience of one of the authors to lead us through and illustrate various points.

Received thought in social work agencies

It is not only traditional casework theory, with its roots in Freudian personality theory, that has influenced developments in social work for the past thirty years; many other strands have also been observed. One concerns the current language of social workers, which has been institutionalised in probation departments and social service departments. These departments have themselves developed their own language, where an internalisation of the way an 'everyday social worker' acts is necessary before one becomes a member of the social work establishment.

It is social work institutions which provide primary control by requiring that institutional order should be observed. Underlying social work institutions are their cultural beliefs and norms which have a profound impact upon the behaviour of social workers. Such beliefs and norms of behaviour include the knowledge, myths, and legends to which all practising social workers are exposed in each social work setting. Knowledge, myths, and legends are created and transmitted through office culture and professional groups. Language helps to make this viable. Language makes it possible to transmit meaning and to allow social workers to make sense of their reality and share their experiences together. The new social worker becomes concerned with the knowledge, meanings, and symbols by which the individual social worker is supposed to know himself and the environment of the agency in which he interacts. Thus an understanding of the language of the social work agency is essential for neophyte social workers. Their language and behaviour develop in that culture and in turn begin to reflect some of its basic features.

Experience and knowledge are passed on from one generation of social worker to another. In the bustling and demanding statutory social work agencies, new generations of social workers are confronted by a confusing mass of legislation, forms, clients and workers. The language of the agency is new, and 'constructs immense edifices of symbolic representation that appear to tower over the reality of everyday life like gigantic presences from another world' (Berger and Luckman 1967: 55).

The student social worker, or newly qualified social worker, is under intense pressure to conform to agency norms. Much has been written about socialisation into a variety of professions, including social work (Goode 1957; Hughes 1958; Bucker and Stelling 1977; Dingwall 1977) whilst Scott has written about the power of established professional practices in welfare bureaucracies (Scott 1969).

It is interesting to note the manner in which radicals often become enmeshed in established agency tradition and practice. Rather than run risks which may be costly in career terms the newly qualified worker bends the rules slightly to champion the little man against the vast machinery of the state and indulges in 'middle class banditry' (Pearson 1975a). When key agency tasks such as report writing are undertaken it is the traditional norms of the agency which prevail above all else – the new arrival conforms and writes reports in the approved 'house style' (Davies and Knopf 1974). Even the conclusions of the reports of workers of a more radical bent are very similar to those of more experienced 'traditionalists' (Hardiker 1977). The apparatus and language of the agency apparently innocuously but insidiously infiltrate the thinking and language of newcomers to social work. They work with 'a caseload', compile 'records', do 'home visits', undertake 'office interviews'. They do not describe their caseload as people but as 'cases' or 'clients'; the term 'home visit' is used, which becomes shorthand language for visiting people in their home; 'office interviews' becomes shorthand language for seeing people at the office. 'Interviews' and 'relationships' are the terms used, instead of the more prosaic and earthy ones, 'talking to people' and 'getting to know people'. All these linguistic devices distance workers from clients while the evidence is that generally the closer workers are to their training, the less they are steeped in the office culture, the less set they are in their attitudes (Day 1981). It is no exaggeration to suggest that the labelling of client/worker interactions described above carries with it the dangers of reifica-

37

tion, of treating people in non-human terms. Social relations become confused; face-to-face contacts between human beings begin to take on the appearance of contact between things; terminology and language place a shield between worker and client.

Received thought in probation and after care

Upon entering a probation and after-care agency it becomes clear that any new worker soon confronts a large caseload, limited resources, and restraints imposed by agency bureaucracy. The agency has to restrict access to certain services despite the needs of clients and, in turn, it sets its employees work priorities. Some of these are set out officially in the agency documentation. Others are communicated to each worker by others in unofficial ways, by hidden unwritten rules, and the use of an 'unofficial' language.

For example, in the work experience of one of the authors, it quickly became apparent that certain 'categories' of clients carried with them some negative connotations. 'NFA' was one particular example. 'NFA' means a person of no fixed abode. In fact this term was usually applied to a person who had recently arrived in the area and had no accommodation. The term had very negative connotations for experienced probation officers. It was known that the worker would begin contact with such clients unexpectedly, because all officers were on the 'NFA' list and could never be sure when they might next be called upon to help. 'Help' in this case often meant responding to clients pleading for urgent financial and accommodation aid. The officers concerned were often resigned to the ever-changing circumstances and lifestyle of such clients, which frequently involved vagrancy, drinking, and 'difficult personalities'. Often the officers approached such encounters in the anticipation that NFAs were likely to be the more hostile and uncooperative clients; this was reflected in the limited enthusiasm and commitment which officers frequently displayed in their work with such men. The end result was that these clients tended to receive an inferior service. They were also depersonalised by being described by officers in terms such as 'he's an NFA' or 'one of my NFAs'. It is very important to emphasise that the probation officers concerned were not incompetent, harsh, or uncaring. Rather the *modus operandi* of the agency was to provide a somewhat different service to NFAs. As a newly qualified probation officer one quickly acquired the meaning and values associated with the term NFA; it had slightly irregular, rejective connotations and it was impossible not to be affected by the abbreviation.

Another term used by probation officers was 'vol after care' (Voluntary After Care). It was known that the agency gave unofficial low priority to after-care work. Such work was rarely discussed with senior probation officers and the relevant records were rarely examined. Furthermore, the probation officer was not directly accountable to a court or any institution beyond the probation service. As a result Voluntary After Care clients moved to the back of the probation officers' filing cabinet. Contact with such clients was infrequent and was sometimes neglected. The term 'vol after care' denoted limited work, occasional visits to prisons, and letters rather than face-to-face contact; often with only limited possibilities of meeting the client in the community; often at a far distant point. The result was that Voluntary After Care was a term which tended to reify the men and women clients concerned, to reduce them to flimsy paper and cardboard files. If to society they were 'out of sight, out of mind', the same comment might be made about many probation officers' attitudes to them. Once again it is important to stress that this was not because officers were uncaring, rather that the underlying feelings in the worker were those of resignation and even fear and trepidation. Therefore this was one area of work which could be 'legitimately' neglected amidst a sea of activity, almost with agency consent.

If 'vol after care' clients were 'out of sight, out of mind' to the officers, there were other terms in the language of the probation service which had the opposite significance. 'Parole' and 'life licence' were 'categories' which tended to generate anxiety, attention, and concern; a concern that was generated within the agency from the received wisdom of the probation officers. The received wisdom attributed status, seriousness, responsibility, accountability, and incentive to be very careful about fulfilling one's obligations. Parole clients and their records were likely to be more regularly discussed with senior officers and involved frequent reporting to outside bodies, notably the Home Office. The connotations of 'parole' were impressive and demanding. The intervention and control of the probation officer were highlighted as, indeed, were the elements and requirements controlling him. Sometimes, also, clients were expected to be less co-operative in these contexts.

All these factors clearly influenced the behaviour and attitudes of probation officers even before they established contact with the clients concerned. They therefore heightened and sharpened the expectations and practice in such situations. In this way the every-day agency language actually undermined some of the traditional core values of social work, such as individualisation and respect. On occasions workers were swamped by agency labels and their negative connotations.

In addition the language used often undervalued practical help that might be offered or suggestions on new ways of doing things made by the new officer. The new arrival, the initiate, found it increasingly hard to be approachable and to 'act natural' (Hugman 1977). While the intention may have been to view clients as fellow citizens in accordance with BASW dictates (BASW 1980), in actual fact the worker was removed from possible positions of equality with clients by several influences. The more down-to-earth aspects of helping were undervalued and it was only through hard and sometimes bitter experience that the new entrant began to appreciate the importance of material help such as money, and, just as importantly, the value of sharing activities with clients such as coffee, drinks, sporting events, and other types of informal contact which can counter the hazy dictates of 'control-led emotional involvement' – one of the decaying cornerstones of traditional casework. Even physical contact when clients faced great distress was discouraged. A statement drawn from a social work student illustrates what we mean:

> Four interviews ago I sat and watched a woman cry: before that I would have put my arm around her, now I don't. It's a detached reasoning process, before it was all emotional. I can separate out the fact that I am there to help and not to gratify my own emotions.
>
> (Cited in Heraud 1981: 104)

In the experience of one of the authors who was employed in Probation and After-Care, while attempts were made to 'accept', to stress 'confidentiality', and allow the mother of a Borstal boy to pursue 'self-determination', she was far more concerned about the ability of the worker to offer her a lift and accompany her on a visit to her son at a nearby Borstal. The language of the agency tended to undervalue action and overvalue ideas and words to the extent that the newly qualified worker could be immobilised and discouraged from offering practical help.

Clients certainly sensed all of this. For the more dyed-in-the-wool client a long series of interviews was no substitute for the workers' presence at a court appearance. Endless hours of conversation meant little to many clients. Time spent with them outside court and a few minutes of positive comment by the worker in court to convince a doubting judge or magistrate were perceived as far more significant and meaningful.

Highly educated graduates were not valued for their education or intellectual ability. Their use of language was likely to be as abrupt and uncaring on occasions as anyone else's. The call of food, the demands of leisure, sometimes overwhelmed the niceties of professional language and labels. One family recalled the regular 4.30 p.m. line of their worker more clearly than anything else she appeared to have said, 'Well it's time I must be going now. I've got to have my tea!' Message sent and understood! But there is another side to the coin. For example, a family who were long established and well known to the agency and had been involved with a long line of workers recalled one incident which stood out above all. This concerned a young female worker who, wet through and soaked to the skin, had asked if she could eat her sandwiches at their house. This one act of simple and ordinary proportions seemed to have meant more to the family than hour after hour of ventilation and counselling with other social workers.

All of this seems to suggest that plain language and a lack of officiousness are much appreciated by clients. Yet to concentrate only upon the clients' perception of received ideas and codes is to give a one-sided picture. In particular, it neglects the important function of occupational integration that received ideas, codes, and protocol perform for workers who are often harassed and over-burdened with heavy caseloads. A study undertaken in the mid 1970s revealed that probation officers spent only around 9 per cent of their time in clients' homes (Davies and Knopf 1974) and it has been estimated that some social workers spend only around 33 per cent of their time outside the office (Satyamurti 1979). The office and its ethos were often used as a shelter, a safe haven, a warm and secure womb where workers could feel a degree of security, largely untouched by outside influences and other professionals. Despite some tensions the majority of probation officers thought they 'spoke the same language'. The anxiety, frustrations, and tensions of work were shared overtly or covertly with colleagues who were used to providing general support. The shared tasks of the office meant that a common bond was established and language was used which might have been impenetrable to outsiders. Clients, magistrates, magistrates' clerks, lawyers, general practitioners, Department of Health and Social Security officials, housing officials, and the police were all excluded from this in-house language, although some were discussed as objects of fun or abuse.

The concern with agency requirements such as records provides a good example. 'Records' was a word which carried a number of meanings. They were the subject of guilt, anxiety, and even pride in some cases. Assessments of the professional competence of probation officers were to some extent based on the manner in which they compiled their records. This played a significant part in a worker's progress towards confirmation around the end of the first year of employment and also contributed towards assessment of his or her capacities for promotion to the post of senior probation officer. At times discussions about records were more likely to be heard than any intense discussion of client problems. Comments about the assessment and ongoing sections of the records abounded. Similar comments could be made about court reports, as so much of the officers' time was concerned with preparing them – around 25 per cent according to some studies (Davies and Knopf 1974). Allocation of reports and allocation of clients were other items of discussion. Sometimes the haphazardness of allocation was bemoaned and senior officers became the subject of stereotypical jokes. This is perhaps most significant of all. Agency discussions were very much focused upon records, reports, and the alleged inadequacies of senior workers, leaving very little space for discussing clients. When this did occur it was often conducted in negative terms.

The language of the organisation, the talk of the office, was not based upon casework principles, counselling attitudes, psychosocial approaches, or the language of care. It was based on discussion of office procedure, office bureaucracy, and office gossip. It was hard for any worker not to participate in gossip. If someone wanted to voice anxiety, annoyance, frustration, or fear they would do so knowing that they would usually receive a sympathetic hearing. It was the demanding and difficult clients who usually received attention of a negative kind and sometimes delivered in scathing language. Clearly workers needed to give vent to pent-up feelings and pressures and it was natural to do so. What is worth noting is that most of these expressions of feelings took the form of outpourings, not necessarily constructive or purposeful discussions about assessment and future directions for helping. The language of casework was often too serious or pretentious. Of course, such comments can be seen as opportunities for hard-pressed workers to obtain relief, but at the same time a certain degree of incongruity is revealed between the intent, the values, the professional aspirations of these workers, and the actual behaviour and language they used with each other. Respect, individualisation, and non-judgemental attitudes were not always evident in the manner in which workers discussed their work. The language used was often of a different nature: lacking in respect, judgemental, and based on stereotypes.

We stated in our introduction that it is essential to regard individuals as skilled, knowledgeable, and creative agents in social life. Our discussion of received thought in traditional social work may have given the opposite impression, i.e. the impression that individual values and actions are mechanically determined. We want to state yet again that it is essential to recognise the twofold action of language and received ideas: they are both constraining and enabling. Our example of the unofficial culture in a probation office illustrates one aspect of this very clearly. The workers evidently operated here in the context of powerful received ideas, codes, and conventions which certainly constrained social values and social action. Yet this did not stop them from subverting official relations and reinterpreting received ideas, codes, and conventions in new and sometimes quite radical ways. Two points must be made. In the first place, this process of subversion was heavily qualified. It did not go 'all the way'. The workers were certainly capable of conforming to official requirements when they had to. Indeed they used considerable skills and interpretative expertise to judge those occasions when the subversion of official ideas and codes were 'safe'. The second point is that this unofficial culture was restricted to the custodians of the official culture. Only the probation officers in the office when the heat was off would defuse the pomposity and seriousness of official received ideas and jargon. It was not acceptable for clients or other work groups linked to the probation service to enter fully the unofficial culture. This right was reserved for fellow probation officers only. In this way the workers asserted their right of possession of the official culture of received ideas and jargon which, after all, was the basis of their livelihood. The process also reinforced occupational integration.

This chapter has not sought to give a complete, full-scale picture of received ideas in social work. In keeping with the general tenor of the book, we have sought to alert social workers to practice and theory issues relating to 'discourse' which, too often, are passed over in silence. We take the view that traditional social work is not the seamless web of logic and enlightened practice that some social work educators would have us believe. Nor do we think that it is the best compromise that can be achieved under present-day conditions. This arrangement of material resources and received wisdom that we call 'traditional social work' contains much that is half-born, improbable, not fully thought through. Ideas like 'respect', 'individualisation', 'trust', 'self-determination', and 'acceptance' are so multidimensional as to be virtually meaningless.

A language may be said to be exhausted when those who speak it no longer have to think about what they are saying but merely recite worn-out slogans and formulas. Certainly, radical social work takes the view that this is the position in traditional social work. Radicals maintain that the exhaustion of language is evident in the fact that the jargon seems irrelevant or inadequate to clients' problems. The focus on case studies and individual problems deflects attention from the structural causes of social and economic problems in class society. All of this is reflected in a 'steady as you go' approach to social change. Traditional social workers are said to see social reform as a piecemeal and gradual process. Little can be accomplished overnight. Only in the long term can the precise and experienced use of therapeutic techniques and specialist knowledge modify the behaviour of clients and, through this, change society. From a radical standpoint this is not the language of reform but the language of resignation. Under it the horizon of the long term constantly shifts. Fundamental social and economic change is ground down into a series of minor and peripheral adjustments in the lives of individual clients. Viewed from the perspective of the individual social worker or the individual client, these adjustments may be of considerable importance. But viewed from the perspective of society as a whole they leave the social and economic fundamentals undisturbed. For this reason, radicals criticise traditional social workers for playing an ideologically dubious role. They reject traditional social work for perpetuating the existing conditions of patriarchy and class inequality in capitalist society.

2

The Marxist alternative

The late 1960s and early 1970s witnessed a number of searing attacks on the language, values, and practices of traditional social work. Although these works did not belong to the Marxist mainstream they nevertheless posed critical ideas which had a definite Marxist ring to them. For example, Brager and Barr (1967), Briar (1968), and Titmuss (1969) criticised traditional social work for perpetuating restricted notions of need and care, and, by extension, neglecting the structural dimensions of personal problems. With Heraud (1970) and Richan and Mendelsohn (1973) they suggested that the language and methods of traditional social work were faulty. To be more specific traditional social work was said to mystify the causes of client distress and to offer bogus solutions to clients' problems. For example, Richan and Mendelsohn (1973: 45) affirmed that 'social work has elected *not* to deal with the conditions that cause poverty. Instead, it has isolated certain emotional aberrations as a cause of poverty and has evolved a psychotherapeutic mode for its treatment' (their emphasis). Here, as in other critical texts of the time, traditional social work was attacked for peddling pious theories that had little to do with the way in which people actually live or with the problems they actually encountered.

Critical criminology and, in particular, labelling theory provided a powerful theoretical framework to articulate these objections. Becker's (1963) concept of 'the outsider' fitted well with many social workers' spontaneous feelings about their clients. Moreover, his notion of social reaction and the construction of deviance seemed to explain the disquiet that afflicted many social workers in witnessing processes of arraignment and sentencing in the juvenile and criminal courts. The writings of Lemert, Doug-

las, Kitsuse, and Matza[1] supplied social workers with ammunition
to fire against the orthodox, positivist, traditional social work
'truths' of the time. Moreover, the labelling perspective showed
clearly how meaning is produced by power and how the use of
language can lead to stereotyping and regulation. In Britain the
magazine *Case Con* was an important switchboard for advancing
and disseminating ideas and alternative forms of theory and practice. Casework, in particular, was singled out as the classic example of all that was narrow, blinkered, and deluded in social work.

Although these radical writings did much to illuminate processes of regulation and control in social work, they were bound by
inherent limitations. As the 1970s and 1980s unfolded these limitations became impossible to ignore. A number of points have
been made. We shall concentrate on the three main ones here
and, for ease of description, we shall list them in summary form:

(1) The eclecticism of radical social work produced a fatal weak-
     ness in the development of theory. Radicals drew on argu-
     ments made in critical studies of mental illness, incarceration,
     the family, delinquency, homosexuality, the oppression of
     women, etc. Taken one by one, these arguments were often
     clear and penetrating. However, they did not add up to a
     coherent theoretical position. Rather, blanket criticism as
     opposed to constructive criticism was the order of the day.
     As Yelloly (1987: 18) comments, 'it was easier to see what
     radical social work was *against* than what it stood *for* in terms
     of alternative practice' (her emphasis).
(2) Radical social work operated with a one-sided view of power.
     Indeed, power was equated with control. For example, the
     standard criticism of traditional social work was that it simply
     functioned to control the client and block progressive change.
     Radical social work cast the client automatically in the role
     of the victim, traditional social workers were portrayed as
     the henchmen of the repressive state, and radical social work-
     ers were sometimes referred to as 'bandits' (Pearson 1975b).
     This is crude stuff. It assumes that the language of radical
     social work inherently produces truthful meanings and that
     the practice of radical social work is intrinsically realistic,
     precise, and effective. These assumptions became increasingly
     difficult to defend as social work became systematically
     exposed to the work of Marx, neo-Marxism, and Weber and
     the writings of Foucault on 'micro-power'.

[margin annotation: Eclecticism.]

[margin annotation: Crude social control.]

46

(3) The philosophy of immediate action was prominent in the self-image of radical social work. However, it proved impossible to build consensus between the interests of the various client groups which radicals represented, e.g. women, ethnic minorities, the handicapped, offenders. By itself, radical social work was condemned as being capable of achieving only a 'welfare rights' type of mentality, i.e. a form of political struggle which aimed to wring more resources from the state for underprivileged target groups, while the system itself remained intact.

The rediscovery of Marx

The 1960s and early 1970s were also a time in which Marxist theory began to make significant inroads into social work. The reasons for this are complex. To begin with, the response of western Marxists to the crisis in Marxism touched upon many areas of relevance to social work. The crisis was caused by the apparent falsification of key propositions in Marxist theory. Thus, in the three volumes of *Capital* and elsewhere, Marx set out the economic and political case for the inevitable collapse of capitalism. Marx argued that the main reasons for the necessary failure of the system were: the 'ruinous' inefficiency and instability of the unregulated market; the tendency for the capitalist class to shrink through intensified competition and the consequent rise in the number of bankruptcies; the polarisation of classes and the intensification of class antagonism; the increasingly repressive nature of the capitalist state; and the growth in numbers and miseries of the unemployed, 'the reserve army of labour'. In the event, capitalism proved to be far more resilient than Marx had predicted. Apart from the Bolshevik breakthrough in 1917, workers' revolutionary movements have suffered a series of humiliating setbacks. Anderson (1983: 15) writes of 'three waves of defeat': first, the snuffing out of proletarian insurgency in Germany, Austria, Hungary, and Italy between 1918 and 1922; second, the collapse of the Popular Front in Spain and France during the late 1930s; third, the breakdown of resistance movements led by mass Communist and Socialist parties in western Europe between 1945 and 1946. Moreover, the sole example of revolutionary 'success', namely the USSR, very evidently congealed rapidly into a repressive party state, far removed from Marx's vision of Communism[2].

As for the capitalist countries, the 'New Deal' form of politics and the post-war reconstruction of the economy seemed to turn out the lights on the prospect of working-class revolt.

In summary then, western Marxists appeared to face a situation in which Marx's theory was no longer relevant to the historical and structural conditions of the advanced industrial societies. How did they respond? And in what ways did this response relate to social work? Let us start with the first question. We shall make five points.

In the first place, western Marxists recognised that the corner-stone of the new system was the state. It was the vastly expanded role of the state in economic ownership and management and the administration of welfare that acted as a key prop in giving the appearance of rational order and steady progress in the west. The extension of health care, unemployment benefit, pension entitlements, housing policy, and state education created the impression of a caring state. Moreover, this impression was carried forward by a progressive fiscal policy and programme of redistributive justice (e.g. 'The New Frontier' and 'The Great Society' in the USA) which aimed to lessen the impact of economic and social inequality.

Secondly, western Marxists maintained that the appearance of order, progress, and justice was nothing other than that: *an appearance*. They pointed out that the working class had not withered away. Poverty and class oppression were still real. The system had changed, but the fundamentals remained intact. Furthermore, the self-congratulatory tone of the western governments on their achievements in welfare provision was dismissed as hopelessly parochial. Capitalism, it was said, must be regarded as a world system of domination. Western affluence is partly built on Third World poverty and hunger.

Thirdly, the corollary of the preoccupation with appearance and illusion was a renewed interest in Marx's original concept of ideology. In a famous passage from *The German Ideology* Marx and Engels (1970: 64) declare that 'the ideas of the ruling class are in every epoch the ruling ideas i.e. the class which is the ruling *material* force in society, is at the same time its ruling *intellectual* force' (their emphasis). Received ideas of 'justice', 'rights', 'care', 'need', etc., are seen as weapons of class control. The administration of welfare is designed to engineer the compliance of the working class.

Fourthly, a great deal of attention was devoted to the new

technologies of cultural integration in the era of state capitalism. The management of compliance was not simply regarded as an effect of state power. Rather, advertising, television, and the lesser media were credited with manufacturing consumer conformism. Marcuse (1964: 78) wrote gloomily of the spread of the 'Happy Consciousness', i.e. 'the belief that the real is rational and that the system delivers the goods'. Horkheimer (1947: 142) meditated on 'all of the ingenious devices of the amusement industry [which] reproduce over and over again banal scenes that are deceptive, because the technical exactness of reproduction veils the falsification of the ideological content.' These writers argued that consumers participated 'willingly' in their own enslavement. The more one consumes the less one owns of oneself and the more one is indebted to the pull of the market. Mass consumerism is seen as being akin to a kind of anaemia: the blood of the consumer is sucked into the market leaving a passive, docile, stunted creature in its wake.

Finally, the Marxist response to current economic, political, and social conditions revitalised the Marxist study of history and communication. On history, the works of Thompson, Hill, Hobsbawm, Hilton, and others[3] heightened consciousness of class and class struggle in capitalist society. As for communication, the studies of Adorno, Horkheimer, Bloch, Della Volpe, the Barthes of *Mythologies*, Williams, and others[4] did much to clarify the repressive, totalitarian aspects of language and meaning in class society.

The response of western Marxists to the crisis can therefore be said to have been systematic and thorough. In what ways did it relate to social work? It occurs to us that the following points are worth making.

For a start, it must be said that Marxism was attractive to many social workers because it provides a more comprehensive and systematic model of the causes of social problems. What traditional social workers treat as private problems which 'belong' to the isolated client, Marxists treat as the public problems of a repressive class system. Marxist concepts of production, class, alienation, ideology, and the state appeared to have the capacity to integrate the perennial scattered problems in social work, e.g. poverty, family conflict, mental illness, bad housing, and personal isolation.

In the second place, Marxists claim that their theory is more objective and more truthful than rival theories. Marx's historical

achievement, ventured Engels on the occasion of his funeral oration at Marx's graveside[5], was the discovery of 'the special law
of motion governing the present-day capitalist mode of production
and the bourgeois society that this mode of production has
created'. Marxism, in short, is credited with scientific socialism.
This involves a materialist and dialectical conception of reality.
By materialism is meant a philosophical approach which views
matter as the ultimate reality; all consciousness is said to be
shaped by material relations. By dialectical, as we stated in our
introduction, is meant a conception of the world which recognises
that all things are in motion and, because of this, are contradictory
and changeable. Marxism therefore encourages a critical attitude
not only to the language and received ideas of bourgeois society,
but also to the language and theoretical tradition of Marxism.

This brings us to our third point. A regular criticism of social
work is that it is all talk and no action. Social workers are said
to be engulfed in an endless round of bargaining over the meanings
and values of words and deeds. As Cohen (1985: 185) remarks,
'social workers devote a great deal of tortuous self-reflection in
deciding whether what they are doing is authority, influence,
persuasion, advice, exhortation, intervention, enforcement, regulation, sanctioning or alas, after all, just "plain control".' Traditional social work, in particular, is said to be unable to move
beyond the language of relativism in approaching social problems.
This is because it is regarded as incapable of transcending the
system of class inequality which causes client distress and produces the monotonous social problems that social workers face.
In contrast, Marxism claims to be the real *science* of society. Central
to this is the idea that social workers can use Marxist theory to
make value-free judgements which are more truthful and effective
than any rival form of social work.

Another, closely related, point which is relevant in explaining
the growth of Marxist social work refers to Marxist programma-
tics. Traditional social work aimed to attain positive social change
through the relief of distress for individual clients and through
maintaining social equilibrium. Radical social workers defined
positive change in terms of winning more resources for underprivileged and oppressed groups and raising client consciousness.
However, it aims to use class rather than sectarian divisions to
transform society:

For the Marxist, the *ultimate function* of social work must be

to raise community, and thus ultimately political, consciousness by exposing the assumed class nature of existing society
at both the local and national level. The greater the 'awareness' the greater the potential for conflict between working-
class activists and 'authority'[6]

(Pritchard and Taylor 1978: 85; their emphasis)

The Marxist programme of action is therefore geared towards
collective organisation and full-scale transformation of society
through collective action.

Our fifth point is that the western Marxist response tackled an
institution which is of the utmost importance to social work in
advanced society: the state. The main employer of social workers
is the state. By casting the state in the role of the administrator
and manipulator of class consciousness, western Marxists posed
an unnerving challenge for state personnel, not least for social
workers. For it undermined the occupational self-image in social
work of a carer, helper, and enabler. Instead social workers were
portrayed as agents of class control. Althusser (1971) describes
them as a vital wing of the state apparatus. Of course, not every
social worker drawn to Marxism accepted this view. As we shall
see, they developed critical positions which portrayed social
workers more positively. However, it did enable Marxist social
workers to engage in the moral condemnation of the welfare state
from a rigorous theoretical position, and this in itself was a fillip
to the spread of Marxist social work.

Finally, there is the question of Communism to consider.
Marxism is about creating a higher form of society, a form which
enables the free and full development of human capacities. As
Marx put it

Communism is the *genuine* resolution of the conflict between
man and nature and between man and man – the true
resolution of the strife between existence and essence, between objectification and self confirmation, between freedom
and necessity, between the individual and the species. Communism is the riddle of history solved, and it knows itself
to be this solution.

(Marx 1964: 135; his emphasis)

Communism is a society without class contradictions and without
illusions. For social workers plagued with the monotonous prob-

51

lems of inequality, personal isolation, and thoughtlessness for others, this is an attractive vision. Certainly, its power to arouse idealistic, humanitarian motives in the social worker should not be underestimated.

Received ideas and Marxist social work: three positions

We have argued that Marxists contend that the whole of capitalist society is in the grip of received ideas. Class illusions and, in particular, the ideology of the welfare state form the context in which social workers must struggle. Marxists are quite sober in their assessment of the massive task of collective organisation and socialist reconstruction facing them. However, they also maintain that the theory and language of Marxism produces a more accurate and truthful form of social work which will enable them to overcome resistance and opposition. Thus, Corrigan and Leonard (1978: 64) comment that 'in political, social, and economic terms, production lies at the very root of an understanding of the working class, capitalism and of the individual and social problems caused by that mode of production.'

Although this view of theory and language is common to all Marxist contributions in social work, it is true that it has been developed to carry different theoretical significance and practical implications by different Marxist writers. Corrigan and Leonard, we suggest, adopt a contradictory position on the role of social work in capitalist society. This may be contrasted with the work of other Marxist authors working in the field, notably Galper, Bailey and Brake, Althusser, Ginsburg, Phillipson, and Simpkin. There is a marked tendency in the literature to treat Marxist social work as a uniform, undifferentiated category of theory and practice. We believe that this tendency is wrong, and we shall break with it radically in this book. It is our contention that there is not one tradition in Marxist social work but three[7]. These are as follows:

(1) *The progressive position:* social work is seen as a catalyst for social change. This is because social workers typically work with clients who are poor and working class, i.e. members of the most exploited class under capitalism. Social workers are therefore well placed to harness and raise working-class con-

sciousness and transform the nature of class society (Galper 1975; Bailey and Brake 1975; Simpkin 1979; Ginsburg 1979).

(2) *The reproductive position:* social work is identified as an indispensable part of the capitalist state machine. It functions to produce, maintain, and reproduce working-class subordination. Social workers are the 'soft cops' of the capitalist state (Althusser 1971; Skenridge and Lennie 1978; Müller and Neusüss 1978).

(3) *The contradictory position:* social work is held both to reproduce and undermine the conditions of class society. It acts as an instrument of class control, and also creates the conditions for the liquidation of class domination (Corrigan and Leonard 1978; Gough 1979; Phillipson 1982; Jones 1983; Leonard 1984).

These positions reflect different judgements on the capacities of Marxist social work and the tasks facing Marxist social workers. In the next three sections of the chapter we aim to elaborate these differences by examining each position systematically and at length. We begin with the most optimistic of the three positions: the progressive position.

The progressive position

Progressive Marxists maintain that capitalist society is based in the organised and systematic oppression of the working class by the capitalist class. In this situation traditional social work is identified as part of the machinery of class control: 'It strengthens this society's repressive characteristics ... At the root of (traditional) social work theory and practice are conservative, or systems conserving assumptions about individuals, the society, and the ways in which change occurs in society' (Galper 1975: 88).

Traditional received ideas of client care, help, counselling, direction, empathy, etc., are rejected as euphemisms for the regulation of the client. However, essential to the progressive view is the conviction that there is nothing inherent in social work which makes it an instrument of class control. Indeed, progressive Marxists insist that social work can be transformed into an instrument of class emancipation.

How is this to be accomplished? The vital objective which progressive social workers set themselves is gaining control of the state apparatus. Once this is accomplished, it is possible to talk sensibly about changing society. At the same time, there is widespread recognition among progressives that control of the state will not be achieved overnight. Making the state the servant of the people's needs and aspirations is acknowledged to be a protracted process. To achieve it social workers are required to wage constructive opposition against social authoritarianism, especially the authoritarianism of the capitalist state. The first arena of struggle is identified as the social work agency. The consciousness of traditional co-workers and clients must be changed by discussion and example. The first task of progressive Marxist social work, then, is consciousness-raising. It consists of helping people to understand that their emotional, occupational, and psychological problems spring from causes which lie outside themselves in the economic and social structure of class society: 'to counteract the effects of opposition the social worker needs to innovate a dual process, assisting people to understand their alienation in terms of their oppression, and building up their self esteem' (Bailey and Brake 1975: 9).

Education is vital. However, it is not an end in itself. The whole point of consciousness-raising, and here the work of Freire (1970) on praxis is frequently cited with approval, is to transform the character of the social work agency. We have to remember that progressive Marxists regard social work agencies as bureaucratic organisations in which clients are routinely stereotyped and stigmatised. Against this, progressive Marxists support moves to democratise agency relations. This entails breaking down hierarchical structures and extending the worker/client partnership in policy formation and decision-making. The aim is to build a genuinely participative form of social work which brings the client in at every stage of theory and practice (Galper 1975; Bolger *et al.* 1981). One rider to this is the rejection of professionalism in social work. Progressive Marxists associate the move to professionalise social work, which has asserted itself strongly in the last two decades, with a growing sense of distance between the worker and the client. This is expressed in several ways, e.g. the growth of jargon in the language of social workers; the restriction of access to clients in department buildings; the increasing importance of professional qualifications as a condition of employment and promotion in agencies; the development of a code of ethics to regulate practice. All of this, it is claimed, has driven a wedge between the worker and the client. It has made the task of appraising client need and solving client problems more difficult. It is also said to have produced more directive attitudes among social workers. Moreover, by creating the basis for the monopolisation of power over standards of practice and control over entry into the profession, it can act as a drawbridge shutting out all new ideas and innovations which run counter to it.

Two further features of the progressive position must be considered. The first feature refers to collectivism. Progressive Marxist writers on social work fully accept that social workers alone are not strong enough to uproot the rule of capital. For this reason they support collective organisation and action. This means forming strong social work unions. It also means developing organisational links with labour unions outside social work as well as working with client groups. The gradual development of a popular front of class opposition is envisaged. By cultivating the politics of collective organisation the working class will eventually triumph. But once again, we must emphasise that progressive authors are careful to note that this will be a protracted process.

The final feature that we want to draw attention to refers to the demythologising power of progressive language. In all of the progressive texts that we have mentioned there is an amazing self-confidence. Marxism is presented as just the thing to cut a swathe through what is alleged to be the muddled and woolly-minded thinking of traditional social work. It is the real analysis of real problems and, to refer back to Marx's phrase, 'it knows itself to be this solution' (Marx 1964: 135). Perhaps the optimism in the scientific value of Marxism was exaggerated. Certainly, the questions of the ambiguity of language and the waywardness of meaning are handled poorly by Marxists. Indeed, Marxists merely assert that Marxism is more truthful, accurate, and objective than rival theoretical approaches. It has been claimed more than once that the assertion does not benefit from being put to the test.

We have now reached the point where it is necessary to examine the progressive position critically. Our discussion is not intended to be exhaustive. However, we do want to point to some acute weaknesses in the progressive position which, we maintain, severely damage its credentials as an alternative form of social work.

We begin with the progressive thesis that social workers are well placed to raise the consciousness of working-class clients. The basis for this is the conviction that Marxist social work theory produces real and solid insights into the problems of working-class clients. However, there is evidence that the working class regards the occupation of social work with suspicion. For example, Rees (1978) found that popular attitudes to social work are often hostile and reactionary. There is a general lack of clarity as to what social workers actually do. Many clients see them as remote and authoritarian figures. The awareness that social workers have statutory powers to remove the individual from the family is more highly developed than an awareness of the counselling and support services in social work. The high trust relations between the worker and the client are not an established or automatic feature of social work encounters. Progressive writers underestimate the layers of prejudice, ignorance, fear, and suspicion in the public imagination that must be dismantled before collective action can begin to shake the foundations of the system.

This brings us to our second point. The progressive position mounts an impressive and moving case for using state social work as a key instrument in creating a more rational and humane society. Galper (1975: 197) maintains that the social worker possesses considerable tactical advantages in switching the resources of the state from repressive to emancipatory practices. This is because work relations in the agency office make it 'unlikely that he or she will be charged with being an outside agitator'. In our view this argument makes excessive claims in respect of the power and freedom of social workers to act in ways which are seriously radical within the state apparatus. We do not doubt that some progressive Marxists will be ready to stake everything, including their jobs and the security of their families, in order to follow their radical aims. However, to suggest that all social workers will do this is ingenuous in the extreme and ignores some basic facts of sociology. Foremost among these is the fact that for the bulk of people living under capitalism, including the majority of social workers, the most vivid and meaningful experiences occur within the framework of the family. Part of the radicalism of the 1960s was the notion that the family is a repressive hang-up of high capitalism which could be dispensed with without much ado. In the event, levels of attachment to family structures have proved to be more intense. Indeed, this fact was skilfully exploited by the New Right in the 1970s and 1980s in their campaign, conducted largely at the level of rhetoric, to defend and nurture family life. At any rate, in our judgement it is implausible to suggest that the mass of social workers will resist redundancy, blacklisting, and family hardship to carry the struggle forward.

Let us refer to two items of recent experience in Britain to support our view. The social work strike in Britain in 1978-9 was not a national strike. Many social workers refused to participate on the grounds that their overriding duty was client care. Others argued that their family responsibilities took priority. The second item refers to the social work dispute over residential staffing in Strathclyde in 1984, which we observed at first hand. Here a similar conflict of loyalties was revealed with social workers being torn between their attachments to co-workers and clients and their family responsibilities.

Leaving aside the question of the basis of viable collectivism between social workers and clients, and the pull of family responsibilities against radical action, there is yet another aspect of progressive thought that we wish to subject to critical scrutiny. This refers to the prospects for constructing genuine progressive social work in one country. The theory and practice of progressive Marxism reveals an astonishing parochialism which makes it quite implausible as a viable theory of social transformation. Capitalism is a world system of domination. All of the struggles to build socialism in one country will come to nought unless they are organised on an international basis.

Why do we state this in such strong language? Let us think through the situation of revolutionary change in one country. Imagine that a workers' movement with representatives of the progressive Marxist position at its head achieved a full-scale transformation of any one of the European countries. After the initial fervour of victory there would be a number of immediate and concrete problems to face. Few countries are self-sufficient. Nearly all rely on international trade for prosperity and growth. The immediate economic effect of Marxist rule would be the withdrawal of international confidence. The remaining capitalist countries would gang up to impose credit restrictions, cease the flow of trade, and withhold investment. The country would be plunged into economic crisis and this would place the Marxist adventure under immense strain. Lest it be thought that our discussion belongs to the realm of imagination, let us recall the political events of the winter of 1976 in Britain. At that time, a Labour government led by James Callaghan buckled under to international pressure and accepted the terms of a huge loan dictated by the International Monetary Fund (IMF). At the heart of these terms was an IMF requirement for Labour to reduce the Public Sector Borrowing Requirement (PSBR). In effect, the international community of capital successfully forced a national Socialist government to change course and introduce large cuts in public expenditure on housing, transport, education, and the social services. The example illustrates how the international dynamics of capital can nip progressive left-wing policies in the bud. The whole question of producing binding international movements of social workers has been ignored by progressive Marxists, to say nothing of the greater question of connecting up these movements to international organisations of the working class.

Finally, we want to develop a point that we hinted at in our discussion of the main features of progressive Marxism. That is, there are real problems with the language of progressive Marxism. The attribution of need is not synonymous with the identification of need. Progressive Marxists may aspire to liberate the talents and energies of all people, yet the unintended effect of their struggle may be to imprison those talents and energies anew. Certainly it is worth remembering that the regimes which currently head the USSR, Poland, Czechoslovakia, Romania, China, and other presently existing 'Socialist' societies began life as movements of progressive Marxism and still see themselves as such.

The reproductive position

The reproductive position maintains that state social work is organised to perpetuate the exploitation and subordination of the working class. It argues that any capitalist state commitment to real care and welfare is illusory. The welfare state is seen as a device instigated by the capitalist class to guarantee the reproduction of a docile labour force. Social work, health care, the whole edifice of social security, are said to exist only so that 'the material existence of wage-labourers is ensured during times when they cannot sell their labour power on the market (sickness, old age, unemployment)' (Müller and Neusüss 1978: 34). Thus the physical condition of wage labourers is controlled so that capitalists have a permanent stock of healthy labourers to draw upon when market opportunity dictates. Thus, too, the hold of capitalist relations of consumption over workers' lives is reproduced. For by supplying the non-working population with a minimum state-approved income in the form of welfare payments, capital ensures that these non-wage-earners can continue the habits of consuming and coveting goods and services. This rope ladder to the market is very important for the reproduction of capitalist society. Ideologically, it signifies the idea of 'caring capitalism'. Economically and socially it ensures that even non-workers (surplus labourers) continue to participate 'voluntarily' in a market system which operates to enslave and dehumanise them.

What role does the reproductive position identify for social work in capitalist society? Unlike the progressive position it argues that social workers have no capability to raise working-class consciousness and promote positive change. Social workers, it is claimed, function to regulate and discipline wage labourers and the non-working population. Through casework and counselling they reinforce dominant (capitalist) stereotypes regarding 'good' marital relations, 'normal' family life, 'proper' standards of public conduct, and 'healthy' consciousness. For the homeless, the unemployed, the delinquents, those variously injured by family experience or experience of urban life in general, social workers act as the 'consuls' of civilised society. They show, in their attitudes, their advice, their words of support and care, that there is a 'normal' life on the other side of poverty, crime, family deprivation, unemployment, and personal isolation. State social work encourages the client to identify with this life and cast off all hostile and negative feelings about society. The consuls of civilised society, then, are said to play an important part in managing compliance among deviant or potentially deviant groups. At the same time they play an important symbolic role in the social integration of 'normal' society. For those in work, the propertied, the ratepayer, the 'normal' person, state social workers are presented as the representatives of caring capitalism. They are proof that 'our' society looks after those who are in genuine need and punishes 'the shirker', 'the scrounger', 'the waster'. In these and other ways, state social work is seen as perpetuating (capitalist) ideas which legitimate the entire system of class repression.

Reproductive analysis concentrates on the ideological role of state social work in policing capitalist society and destroying forms of social life, including forms of radical language, which threaten the maintenance of the system. Social workers are portrayed as agents of class mystification and political control. They pump out the message that society is basically unchangeable, that the best is already being done for those in want, and that poverty is the result of bad luck or personal inadequacy.

From the reproductive perspective, the language of traditional social work is the language of discipline and control. The surface of understanding, kindness, and compassion conceals strong authoritarian sentiments underneath. For example, the term 'care order' is a euphemism for the legal power of the social worker to remove a child from home and confine him or her to an institution. Similarly, the term 'home visit' conjures up a hale and reassuring vision of the social worker contacting the client in the home and discussing his or her problems in a relaxed and informal way. However, the term is also a euphemism for an investigation of the home of the client in order to assemble material for a report. Finally, social workers often justify their decisions by saying that they are 'acting in the best interests of the client'. Yet the client is often excluded from playing any meaningful part in the decision-making process. Instead, real power rests with agents of the state, e.g. social workers, the police, magistrates, and consultants.

Reproductive thought draws heavily on the theoretical writings of the so-called 'structuralist' Marxists, notably Althusser and Poulantzas, who produced a series of key critical works on the capitalist state in the late 1960s and early 1970s. According to these authors, the capitalist state now plays a major role in the ideological and physical subordination of the working class: 'the principal role of the state apparatus is to maintain the unity and cohesion of the social formation by concentrating and sanctioning class domination, and in this way reproducing social relations i.e. class relations' (Poulantzas 1975: 25). According to Poulantzas, social workers are part and parcel of this set-up of class domination.

Althusser's influence is evident in both the tone and substance of Poulantzas's words, especially in the phrase 'state apparatus'. Althusser (1971) divides the modern welfare state into two parts: the Repressive State Apparatus (RSA) and the Ideological State Apparatus (ISA). The RSA consists of the police, the armed forces, the judiciary, and the prisons. Its function is to mobilise the use of legitimate physical force against unruly and disruptive elements in society, i.e. to maintain the rule of capital. The ISA system consists of religious and educational institutions, political parties, trade unions, the mass media, the leisure industry, and state social work. It operates to mobilise guilt, fear, superstition, and a sense of fatalism in the working class. For Althusser, what is distinctive about modern capitalism is that order is maintained largely through symbolic and ideological means. The ISA system has not entirely replaced the RSA system in making people more docile. Repressive forces always lurk in the background. Similarly, it is certainly the case that there is a marked overlap between ideological and repressive functions in many areas of the state machine. Consider the case of state social workers. They are said to participate in the moral regulation of working-class populations through ideological means, i.e. in the use of a received language of 'order', 'health', and 'propriety'. Yet social workers also possess statutory powers which enable them to call on the resources of the RSA system, notably the police, magistrates, the prisons, psychiatric institutions, to subdue or physically remove clients who are graded as being difficult, unmanageable, or at 'high risk'. However, although these repressive aspects are essential to the authority of state social work under capitalism, the basic mechanism of control is ideology.

An important and controversial feature of the reproductive position is its determinism. It argues that the consciousness and actions of social workers are conditioned by their social work training and the social positions which they occupy in social work agencies. In some versions of the reproductive argument social workers are denied any capacity for independent consciousness and critical language, i.e. they are viewed as lacking the freedom to act as they please. For example, 'the ideologies through which social workers reflect their position as agents within a state apparatus, is not a function of the agent's subjective consciousness, but of the place these agents occupy in the social formation' (Skenridge and Lennie 1978: 91). This, it seems, reduces social workers to mere cogs in the capitalist state machine.

Determinism, in the sense in which Skenridge and Lennie use it, implies that human beings are essentially passive creatures. They do not act upon the world, rather the world acts upon them to shape their thoughts, feelings, words, and actions. One important implication of this is that social workers are seen as incapable of understanding or changing the world. As subjects, they simply fulfil the objective requirements of their work position in the capitalist state machine. On this account then, there is no prospect of social workers linking up with the working class to take conscious control of the state apparatus and divert it from coercive to emancipatory practices. Galper's (1975: 142) progressive humanist vision of a revolutionary new society in which 'every person is afforded maximum opportunity to enrich his or her spiritual, psychological, physical and intellectual well being' is rejected as a delusion.

There is truth in the reproductive case. Welfare is mediated through ideology. Social work does involve the moral regulation of the client. 'Care' is used as a euphemism for 'control', 'normality' for 'discipline', 'helping' for 'administration', etc. However, it is also necessary to state that there is much in the reproductive position which is false and one-sided.

To begin with, it presents a monolithic view of the welfare state. According to this, the welfare state is merely a machine for manipulating consciousness and reproducing working-class subordination. We object to this because it ignores the long-term struggle of the workers to achieve welfare rights and treats the working-class client as the mere passive victim of the system. A quite unbalanced view of power is therefore perpetuated. It presents the state as being all-powerful and the worker as being powerless.

Moreover, the reproductive position endorses a very one-dimensional view of social work language. Thus, the language of social work is said to be conformist, authoritarian, and inflexible. It promises the liberation of the client, but only delivers further mystification and control. No doubt this is an effective metaphor of social work language. However, it is essential to insist that it is nothing more than that: a metaphor. Its relation to concrete reality is dubious. In particular, there is no real appreciation of the contradictory nature of social work language. That is, as we stated in our introduction, social work language has a twofold action: it is both enabling and constraining, it expands client options but also conditions them in quite specific ways.

What is more, the reproductive position underestimates the real level of diversity that exists in social work theory. Counselling, task-centred work, the unitary approach, behaviour modification, group work, family therapy, Marxism, feminism, etc., reflect very different positions on client care, analysis, and action in social work practice. This diversity has produced a high degree of critical debate *within* social work. It is certainly much higher than is conveyed by the term 'reproductive social work' which brings to mind a standard and inflexible action.

Finally, there is the question of the meaning of political action. The reproductive position maintains an unbending scepticism towards affirmative visions of social work practice and society. It dismisses them as mere acts of wishful thinking, the articulate utopianism of the hopelessly oppressed. Indeed, the view that political action by social workers is encouraged by the authoritarian state is fully consistent with reproductive analysis, for a measure of dissent gives the illusion of freedom and struggle in social conditions which are regulated scrupulously. Indeed so scrupulous is the process of regulation said to be that the reproductive position concludes that freedom and struggle are objectively denied.

So far in this chapter we have examined the progressive and reproductive positions. We have argued that the progressive position is extravagantly Utopian in its analysis of the power of social work and the prospects for full-scale social change. Moreover, we have criticized the reproductive view for its excessive determinism. The Marxist approach in social work which claims to avoid the snares and delusions of utopianism and determinism is what we call the contradictory position. We have now come to the point in our discussion where it is necessary to examine this position in detail.

The contradictory position

The contradictory position is based in the proposition that 'the welfare state is a product of the contradictory development of capitalist society and in turn it has generated new contradictions which every day become more apparent' (Gough 1979: 152).

The central contradiction is between the ideology of care and the practice of care. The contradictory position recognises the welfare state as a genuine step forward. Yet, at the same time, modern society is said to be based on profound class inequality and, further, the welfare state bears all the birthmarks of this condition. To be specific, it is argued that the welfare system is constrained by the requirements of the capitalist economic system. It cannot fully meet the needs of clients because the labour requirements of the economic system demand that these needs are limited and regulated in order to produce a disciplined work-force. The logic of the system is that if the workers are given too much in the form of welfare benefits they will no longer have an incentive to work. If this incentive is undermined the whole security of capitalist society is placed in jeopardy. Hence, the welfare state is compelled to apply a selective concept of need and a restricted concept of care. In this sense, the welfare state reflects the contradictions between the forces and relations of production which ripple through the whole of capitalist society.

What role precisely does the contradictory position assign to state social work in this context?

> Since its modern origins in the middle of the last century, social work has been one of the many strategies developed and deployed by the ruling class and the state for intervening in the lives of working people ... social work has to be considered as one of the agencies of class control and regulation.
>
> (Jones 1983: 9)

At first sight this looks like a rerun of the reproductive thesis that state social work is to be considered as merely an instrument of class domination. However, this is not the case. Indeed implicitly, and sometimes in very explicit ways, the contradictory position is dismissive of the reproductive standpoint. For example, Corrigan and Leonard (1978: 95) maintain that 'it is too simple to see the State *only* in terms of the reflection of ruling class interests: the State reflects *struggle* as well as the *status quo*' (their emphasis). Similarly, Bolger *et al.* suggest that the concept of contradiction distinguishes the contradictory position inherently from the reproductive position:

> a contradiction means that there are elements of that structure that can only be *fully* realised, can only be fully put into effect, by destroying other elements of that situation. This means that the structure is in *constant tension* since one part of the structure can only be successfully realised at the expense of another.
>
> (Bolger *et al.* 1981: 3; their emphasis)

On this account, social work is not the bottled spider of the capitalist class. Rather, social workers are said to possess some autonomy and discretion in their work activities. The distinction is crucial. By conferring relative autonomy on the state, the contradictory position establishes critical distance from both the reproductive and progressive positions in Marxist social work. If the reproductive position sees the social worker as the henchman of the capitalist class, the contradictory position sees the Marxist social worker as a fifth columnist: working within the system to destroy it. This view is shared by the progressive position. But unlike the progressive position, there is far more emphasis on the dialectical character of all things, and hence a less Utopian attitude to social change. Thus, it is said that, in transforming existing conditions, Marxist social work transforms the conditions of its own existence and so produces a new set of contradictions which act as the incentive for further critical reaction. Even in a society which has undergone radical change in a progressive direction it is acknowledged that there will be new limits and social conflicts. There is no end point to human history and thus no prospect of lasting harmony in human affairs.

These then are the basic presuppositions of the contradictory position in Marxist social work. What of the practical policies applied to social work in order to achieve emancipatory welfare relations? Here there are close parallels with the progressive position. For example, social workers are encouraged to: (a) raise the consciousness of clients and co-workers; (b) build strong social work unions; and (c) forge links with working-class organisations outside social work, especially established trade unions. In addition, a strong argument is made for the increased democratisation of state welfare institutions and services so that public resources are used in favour of clients. Genuine partnership is envisaged, with client representation in the decision-making process in welfare investment, resource allocation, and agency strategy. All of this requires social workers to cultivate consistently positive attitudes towards clients. In the progressive position, social worker/client relationships are discussed in a teacher/pupil framework. The social worker is depicted as using his or her specialist knowledge to guide the client into patterns of effective resistance against the received ideas of capitalist society. Against this, the contradictory position favours open encounters with clients. The social worker must be expected to learn as well as teach. Relationships must be non-directive and display great trust. The social worker and client are required to be not merely critical but also self-critical.

It must be said that the contradictory position makes huge demands on the social worker. 'Float like a butterfly, sting like a bee,' Corrigan and Leonard (1978: 155) tell their social work readers. It is a role which requires practitioners to be constantly vigilant. Developments must be anticipated, opportunities seized, Socialist legality observed, without producing harmful counter-reactions in the Marxist fraternity. The social worker is called upon to be a risk taker and a compromiser; an innovator and a bulwark of client support. It is a role full of conflict, tension, and stress. However, it is also argued that these conditions are not confined to social work. Rather, they are the general conditions of class society. Moreover, it is claimed that the theoretical knowledge which Marxist social workers have at their disposal equips them to manage conflict, stress, and tension positively. Corrigan and Leonard (1978: 151-3) urge social workers to play an 'intellectual' role. This is a loaded word, and certainly one that many social workers feel uncomfortable with. By 'intellectual' Corrigan and Leonard mean a practical theorist of social relations who is able to use theoretical knowledge as a catalyst for collective organisation and action.

This completes our discussion of the main features of the contradictory position in Marxist social work. We now want to move on to a critical discussion of this position. As our starting-point let us take the contradictory viewpoint on class. Although the contradictory position does recognise other forms of struggle under capitalism, notably forms relating to gender and race (see Leonard 1984), the concept of class and the question of class struggle occupy centre stage. Thus, it is said that the three main objectives of Marxist social work are raising working-class consciousness, engendering working-class organisation, and stimulating working-class action. The main difficulty with this line of analysis is that it endows the working class with a real capacity for unified and coherent action which it does not in fact possess. We do not mean to discount the significance of class in society or the social problems which social workers encounter. The point at issue is the capacity of the working class to act, not the existence of that class. As Hindess remarks,

> the use of the term 'class struggle' to refer to certain kinds of collective action (strikes, factory occupations, or whatever) obviously requires the existence of classes in the sense of different categories of persons. But it is one thing to analyse a class as a category of persons, and quite another to treat the class itself as a collective actor engaged in struggles with other collective actors.
>
> (Hindess 1986: 118-19)

It is precisely the practice in the contradictory Marxist position of treating the working class as a collective actor that we are criticising here. Indeed, it might be said that the concept of class has become the central received idea of Marxist social work. That is, it is obediently unquestioned despite the fact that it is inconsistent with observation and experience. We shall come back to this point in the final section of the chapter.

A theory of collective action means nothing without a theory of collective need. The contradictory position indeed endorses a theory of universal needs. For example, the needs for food, health, shelter, sexual satisfaction, open communication, democracy, the company of others, and liberation are said to be basic human needs (see Doyal and Gough 1984; Leonard 1984: 88-90). There is much to admire in this line of argument: the recognition that the needs of the many are repressed under existing conditions; the notion that repression can be changed through vigorous social action; the commitment to extend the satisfaction of need from a privilege of the few to a right of the many, etc. However, the view is also vulnerable to a major objection. That is, it confuses the metaphorical and substantive dimensions of the concept of need. For example, if liberation means anything, it means the capacity to act as one pleases. However, if all action is dictated and justified by personal choice social order is placed in jeopardy. Why is this? If all people have the right to indulge in the liberation of felt needs, some may choose to engage in molesting little children; others may elect to harm the natural environment, steal, engage in acts of physical violence, etc. If the metaphor of liberation is turned into a substantive right which all people have it will lead to some very illiberal, very authoritarian forms of practice. Against this, Marxists will say that the need for liberation cannot be satisfied unless other human needs are also satisfied, notably the needs for open communication, democracy, and the company of others. To do this requires uprooting the rule of capital, since it is capital above all else which distorts human needs and dehumanises people. Again, we find much to admire in this argument. Capitalism is certainly a form of society which encourages personal acquisition, individual envy, and spite to a degree which dehumanises the quality of human life. However, it is futile to imagine that the clock can be turned back. Capitalism cannot be disinvented. The rise and establishment of capitalist forms of life have changed people. These changes will persist even if the economic and political system which gave rise to them disappears. It is, of course, important to add that these changes will themselves be eventually changed by the disappearance of capitalism. However, the form and direction of these changes are by no means a closed question. Certainly, Marxists delude themselves if they believe in the inevitability of the free and full development of all human beings because history is on 'our' side.

To some extent, the dangers of a universal theory of human need are recognised in the contradictory position. For sure, the fundamental proposition of contradictory social work is that all human things are contradictory and hence changeable. Yet in spite of this, even the best writers in the contradictory tradition seem to mistake the end of capitalism for the end of contradiction and the end of illusion. Consider Leonard (1984: 91) who writes that 'the unresolvable contradiction in the lives of most people under capitalism is that whilst social labour is necessary, it is also abstract and does not, for most, allow the expanded development of capacities.' The strong implication of these words is that this contradiction can be solved under another form of social and economic organisation. Moreover, at another point in his discussion Leonard (1984: 207) ventures that 'if we are not to be bounded forever within ideology, within the "objective illusion" of the social relations of capitalism, then we must gain knowledge of these social relations and how they are constructed within our own personalities.' Again the strong implication of this sentence is that it is feasible to organise forms of human life which are 'without ideology'. Now we are aware that in both the passages that we have cited, Leonard is referring to contradictions and ideologies which belong to a specific historical and structural form of social life, namely capitalism. It is perfectly legitimate to imagine other forms of society in which these contradictions and ideologies are absent. In other words, to argue for the end of capitalist contradiction and capitalist ideology is very different from arguing that all contradiction and ideology can be put to an end. However, the silence of Leonard and other writers in the contradictory position on the question of the organisation of higher, non-capitalist forms of social work and society is dismaying. Given the conventions of Marxist discourse, it is obvious that the higher forms in question are Socialism and Communism. The failure of the contradictory position to engage in any serious way with an analysis of relations of need, freedom, and constraint in the presently existing Socialist societies of eastern Europe, China, and elsewhere, is therefore very surprising. For plainly, these relations do not provide auspicious judgements and prognostications for Socialism in the west. In effect, the contradictory position invites social workers to risk everything for Socialism in a historical situation where the only examples of it have infallibly led to terror and repression.

We now come to our final point. The contradictory position is scornful of what it regards as the elitism and irrelevance of traditional social work. Casework, in particular, is regarded as intrinsically authoritarian in its language and content, and superfluous in the insight it brings to the real causes of client suffering. Against this, the contradictory position applies its version of Marxist thought as a genuinely scientific approach to the study of social relations. The social worker is urged to act as a practical theoretician, linking the concrete and immediate problems of the client to the deep structural principles of class inequality and dialectical materialism identified in Marxism. The paradox here is that, in key respects, the use of Marxist theory in social work is alleged to produce the same effects which Marxists disdain in traditional practice. Thus, Marxist social work is said to be authoritarian in its analysis of clients' problems and to stereotype or discount interpretations of social work and social problems which counter the Marxist line. As Cohen observes ruefully:

> Not only are we back to the elitism of the psychoanalytically derived casework – whatever you say, we really know best what your problem is – but we end up with another form of non-intervention or benign neglect: only this time, one reserved for the unfortunate few who refuse to see themselves as the social worker's political allies. What if the client actually wants something like casework? A case of false consciousness, no doubt.
>
> (Cohen 1975: 90)

Thus, as is the case with traditional social work, the language of Marxism in practice treats the client as a mere object of administration. Before a problem is encountered, the language has a solution. If clients lack a vision of their future, the language tells them what their lives should be like. Clients' anger and resentment are projected from themselves or the immediate members of their families to abstract, external forces in social life, notably the class system.

Action and discourse

The conflicts between the three positions in Marxist social work do not arise for accidental reasons. On the contrary, they are the result of the *practical struggle* to apply Marxist theory to real social conditions. Classical Marxism was based in the idea of unity between purpose and action. It was thought that the competent application of Marxist theory would revolutionise society. Working-class action would put an end to mass oppression, alienation, and the brutalisation of labour. It would be the beginning of freedom. This powerful intellectual legacy is evident in the contradictory and especially progressive contributions to Marxist social work. However, the conformity between them is minimal and besides, neither is compatible with the reproductive position. Doubtless these conflicts do much to confirm the vitality of Marxist social work. Yet they also pose a real dilemma. If Marxist social workers cannot agree among themselves on the analysis of social work in class society, how can they expect to persuade others?

This question goes right to the heart of Marxist social work in the modern world. It requires us to consider the viability of class collectivism as the basis for a comprehensive, organised programme of change. In the last section we argued that the contradictory position confuses the metaphorical and substantive dimensions of the concept of need. The same might be said of the progressive and reproductive positions. If human beings really are made up of universal human needs it is quite clear that they have striven to realise them in very different ways. Nowhere is this clearer than in the area of trade unionism. Ironically, the progressive and contradictory positions both see trade unionism as the prerequisite of collective transformation. However, with one or two exceptions, such as 'the events' in France in 1968, trade union collectivism in the European Community and North America has existed as a dream and not a reality. In Britain, for most of the post-war period, the trade unions have engaged in fervent mutual competition. The result is that the trade union movement is now stratified in terms of skill and sectionalised in terms of bargaining power. The wretched isolation of the miners during the long strike of 1984-5 provides copious, heart-rending evidence of the divisions that exist within the British labour force. Trade union solidarity is more highly developed on the European mainland, especially in those countries with strong neo-Marxist political parties, such as Italy, France, Germany, and Sweden. However, even there, the union movements consistently collaborate with capital to increase the system's economic efficiency, for example through wage restraint and participating in productivity schemes. Most trade union leaders regard their overrriding duty as the maintenance of full, high-wage employment for their members. They have tried to take more out of the system rather than changing its economic and social basis.

The question of sectionalism and fragmentation cannot be confined to work relations. It is palpable also in working-class culture. Thus, many working-class people define themselves first and foremost by their gender, race, family responsibilities, regional ties, and leisure pastimes. These attachments are held to be more vivid, indispensable, and meaningful than attachments of class. Social workers, whether Marxist or not, will be very familiar with this. Very few clients think of themselves seriously and consistently as members of the most exploited class under capitalism. They do not submerge their individuality in sentiments of class collectivism. Rather, they see themselves as abandoned mothers, unemployed fathers, blacks who have suffered discrimination, handicapped persons, daughters unable to cope with elderly dependants, abused children, etc. In this connection it is interesting to observe that Leonard (1984), in his most authoritative attempt to produce a viable Marxist understanding of social work and welfare under capitalism, is very thin on examples of successful working-class collectivism in the post-war period. To be sure, the only examples he cites (1984: 206-13) refer to welfare rights groups, e.g. Claimants' Unions, women's consciousness-raising groups, the Liberation Movement of People with Disabilities, and the black anti-racist movement. However, what is distinctive about these groups is not their class character but the limited and particularistic nature of their aims and collective organisation.

It is tempting to see sectionalism and division in working-class life as the result of deliberate policies of divide and rule perpetuated by the all-powerful ruling class. Indeed, the reproductive position argues precisely this case. It is not convincing. As Means puts it:

> working class divisions are not created artificially by the state through such devices as a social work service which focusses on the pathology of the urban poor. These divisions are rather inherent in the day-to-day functioning of capitalism; the quality of life for each worker is dependent upon the success of his struggle for scarce resources and this inevitably leads him into conflict with other members of his class.
>
> (Means 1979: 24)

In other words, sectionalism is not caused by duping workers. On the contrary, it springs from the concrete judgements made by them in their struggle to gain more resources for themselves and their families. Moreover, despite the realisation that mutual competition diminishes the power of the working class to win lasting collective gains, strong pressures work against the translation of the realisation into policy. Beer puts matters well in his commentary on the struggle for resources from the welfare state:

> Because so many are making claims, the claim of no single group can make much difference to the level of public expenditure. Self-restraint by a particular group, therefore, would bring no discernible benefit to it or to any other group, but on the contrary would penalise the self-denying group with a significant loss. Hence, even though the group may recognise the need for all participants to moderate their claims, it will be tempted to raise its own.
>
> (Beer 1982: 30-1)

Beer's words accurately describe how collective bargaining actually works in modern society: sectional interests prevail above collective interests. It does not follow that collective action is therefore a pipedream. There may be circumstances, such as the collapse of the entire economic system, which are propitious to genuine collectivism. All that can be said safely is that these circumstances do not exist now, and their prospects are remote.

Collectivism means action, and the mainspring of action is communication. It is perfectly clear that the three positions in Marxist social work analyse and describe the functions of social work in class society in very different ways. Moreover, embedded in their descriptions is a tacit system of judgements as to what constitutes valid and invalid assumptions, and right and wrong propositions, regarding social work, the working class, and the society which encircles them. This language, or discourse, is important for it shapes not only policies but also the topics which are considered for policy formation. In general, Marxists have paid insufficient attention to discourse. They have assumed that Marxist theory simply reflects reality. That is, it cuts through the ideological distortions and class fabrications of capitalism to the truth of the matter. In short, as we said of progressive Marxism earlier in the chapter, it is credited with digging out real meanings about real things.

We shall take up the question of discourse and social work and examine it in detail in Chapter 4. At this stage in our discussion it is sufficient to note that a long line of western philosophy, from

Nietzsche, Heidegger, Wittgenstein, and Foucault to Derrida, stands in opposition to the proposition that language reflects reality. These writers play up the ambiguity and dynamism of speech and language. Words mean different things to different people, meanings change according to their situation. In brief, meaning, and hence 'truth' and 'reality', are called into question.

There are several ways of illustrating the proposition that the language of Marxist social work fails to reflect reality. However, we propose to close this chapter by using the examples of three received ideas drawn from Marxism: belonging, alienation, and equality of opportunity.

The concept of belonging is central to Marxist approaches to social work. There are humanist and class dimensions to the concept and we shall consider them separately. The humanist dimension of belonging stresses that all individuals feel the need to belong to others. This need is not defended by Marxists on mere emotional grounds. It is also said to be motivated by the quite rational judgement that the health, peace, and livelihood of the individual are interdependent with those of all individuals. Yet the monotonous experience of social workers is to encounter individuals who are abandoned by their families and communities. Indeed, the inadequacies of social policies for the homeless, the disabled, the elderly, and the unemployed suggest that the state has institutionalised the concept of marginality for large categories of the population. Marxist social workers therefore apply an idea of care and practice which is explicitly and widely denied under the actually existing conditions of society. This might be expected to underline the irrelevance of Marxist ideas for the analysis of modern social problems. Far from it. Marxists argue that the denial of belonging is a requirement of the capitalist mode of production. Capitalism, they continue, is a system founded upon possessive individualism. Inevitably, this pits the employer against the worker and worker against worker. Yet from this generalised antagonism a new form of belonging is said to sprout forth.

We now come to the second dimension of the Marxist concept of belonging. For this new form is nothing other than class consciousness. The argument runs like this. The denial of belonging is not a matter of chance, it is systematic. Yet the repeated efforts of capital to divide workers, eliminate their resistance, and accentuate their docility, is said to create the conditions for collective organisation and action. The new sense of belonging is therefore

projected along class lines. Marxism indeed predicts the polarisation of classes. Capital bands together to oppress the workers;
and the workers unite to challenge the rule of capital which denies
them the satisfaction of their innate needs. The reader may judge
where we stand on this account of class belonging by referring
back to our critical discussion of trade union collectivism. In
general, we argue that the concept of class belonging is inconsistent
with what most people actually observe and experience in their
everyday relations. However, it is not the empirical absence of
the concept of class belonging that we must comment upon here.
It is the narrowness of the concept. It is narrow because it neglects
forms of belonging associated with race, disability, age, and above
all gender and sexuality. Marchant (1986) attacks the contradictory position as embodied in the work of Corrigan and Leonard
(1978) for exaggerating the importance of men's work. 'By isolat-
ing production as the central issue,' she writes (1986: 27), 'they
pass over discussion of reproduction.' In some feminist quarters
the sense of belonging which female social workers and clients
can build in discussing male power and female oppression is said
to oust other forms of collective organisation, e.g. forms built on
class or race exploitation: 'Women's opposition to patriarchy',
comment the Birmingham Women and Social Work Group
(1985: 119), 'has neither an immediate parallel in the fight for
socialism, nor reliable allies in male socialists, black or white.'
We shall return to the question of feminism and social work and
examine it at length in the next chapter. Here we simply wish to
emphasise that we live in societies made up of many different
kinds of belonging. The attachments and problems of clients, no
less than those of social workers, are diverse and manifold. The
humanist dimension of belonging in Marxist approaches to social
work, with its global and undifferentiated emphasis, runs aground
and splinters against these powerful divisions.

Another key concept for Marxist social workers is 'alienation'.
'Man' is said to be estranged from his 'natural' self and from his
fellow human beings. The cause of this is located in capitalism
which is alleged to exaggerate individualism, acquisitiveness, and
competition to an unhealthy degree. Literally speaking, we live
in societies which make us sick, and this is exposed quite tangibly
in our physical, social, and emotional lack of well-being. Yet it
is regularly said in criticism of the Marxist concept of alienation
that it explains everything and nothing. For while social workers
will find it easy to give examples of isolation, despair, and estrange-

ment among clients, they are very often tempered with examples
of clients who attest to warm and satisfactory relationships with
members of the family, friends, co-workers, etc. There is, then, a
tension between the Marxist analysis of the objective conditions
of capitalism and the subjective interpretation and feelings of
individuals. Of course, Marxists have dealt with criticisms which
spring from this tension by maintaining that the individual is so
thoroughly alienated that misery is regularly confused with happiness and pain with pleasure. However, this is to attribute false
consciousness to the 'contented' client and to reinforce the 'we
know best' attitude in the administration of welfare which Cohen
(1975; 1985) and others have commented upon. The rather unsatisfactory corollary of this is that the 'contented' client is portrayed implicitly, and sometimes in very explicit ways, as a clueless
automaton. That is, he is unable to make sense of his condition
or is incapable of breaking his dependence on the system which
enslaves him. False consciousness or not, there is substantial resistance in the working class to changing the system fundamentally.
This is evident, as we have already noted in the collaborationist
attitude of trade unions. Moreover, it is further apparent in the
phenomenon of large-scale working-class support for the right-
wing political parties of capital. If these people are alienated,
leading symptoms of their condition are an inherent satisfaction
with the existing system and scepticism about left-wing programmes of change. It is difficult to see how these symptoms can
be rooted out without the use of force and authoritarianism.

Finally, 'equality of opportunity' is another important idea in
Marxist social work. A decent society, Marxists argue, demands
that every citizen should have an equal opportunity to develop
his or her talents to the full. The prerequisite for equal opportunity
is the provision of adequate and universal health care and education. Marxists reject the idea that equality of opportunity is compatible with capitalism. They advocate the collectivisation of property and the abolition of class society as the only way to achieve
real equality of opportunity. Now, it is obvious, and it has been
pointed out on many occasions, that the creation of equal opportunity interferes with liberty. For if equal opportunity is to be
guaranteed, the individual cannot have the freedom to incur only
such obligations and contracts as he or she wishes, or to determine
his or her own free choice. It is still an open philosophical question
whether society should have liberty over equality or equality over
liberty, or indeed, what the mix between the two ought to be.

Clark with Asquith (1985: 55-75) have reviewed the main philosophical positions which bear upon social work and we can recommend their summary as a useful guide to this complicated area. Here we wish simply to observe that equality of opportunity is incompatible with freedom of choice and action. The progressive and contradictory positions in Marxist social work may look forward to the free and full development of all individuals. However, at the present time, no higher form of society is concretely visible.

It would be premature to speak of the end of Marxist social work. The constituency of supporters is too well established, the critical analysis of capitalism too vivid and, in key respects, too accurate. However, despite more than a decade of Marxist writings on social work and forms of intervention in area teams and residential settings, Marxism has not been all-conquering. Indeed it continues to be taught and practised as one approach to social work among others. The failure of Marxism to break the mould, together with the schisms in Marxist theory and practice that we have enumerated in this chapter, embolden us to maintain that the high-water mark of Marxist influence has now almost certainly been passed. The most imaginative and stimulating work in social work in the present day is certainly being done by adopting a thoroughly eclectic attitude to Marxism. It consists of selecting limbs from Marxism and grafting them on to the trunks of feminism, discourse theory, and critical psychology (see for example Marchant and Wearing 1986; Philp 1979; Donzelot 1979; Dorwick 1983). There are stylish and luminous perceptions of social work to be found here. In Chapter 4 we examine aspects of them in the course of our discussion of discourse analysis and social work. However, before reaching that point it is necessary to consider a form of social work which many claim to be *the* critical challenge to traditional social work, surpassing Marxism, discourse theory, critical psychology, and other radical approaches besides. We refer to feminist social work. An account of this movement, its strengths and limitations, is the subject of our next chapter.

3

Women, social work, and feminism

In this chapter we want to explore the received ideas clustered around women in social work. We will use this to examine the contribution of feminist thought to the development of social work theory and practice. Our discussion, like all discussions on women and social work, is fuelled with a deep sense of irony. Social work should be a *cause célèbre* for women – a profession created by women for women. Yet, in reality, women workers operate as the foot soldiers in an army governed by male generals and deal regularly with women clients who are the victims of male oppression. Moreover, as Langan (1985: 28) notes: 'Although most social work clients and most social workers are women, the theory and practice of social work reflect little appreciation of the important question of women's oppression.'

'Dear girls'

A lasting achievement of feminism is to show unequivocally that gender is a form of communication. We go through life not merely as individuals but, crucially, as men and women. The work and leisure experiences that are available to us are closely related to our gender.

This is manifestly true of social work, and it can be illustrated in a number of ways. Consider, for example, received ideas about the 'special qualities' of women workers. Women are seen as 'natural' carers and nurturers. Their talents tend to be defined in passive terms. Women are thought to be good listeners, good at soothing troubled clients, and reliable in following orders efficiently. The active roles of decision-making and taking command are basically seen as a male preserve. Not surprisingly, there are more men than women in senior social work posts. Consider further the experience of women who do make it to the top in social work. In ways that have no counterpart in the experience of male managers, they are subject to a patronising language which labels them as essentially dependent creatures ('my dear', 'old love', 'girls'). Christine Walby (1987: 10-11), a Director of Social Services, lists some of the most common male reactions to working with women in senior management:

(1) Women who attend meetings/negotiations with a male colleague are automatically assumed to be his secretary or subordinate.
(2) Women in authority are often treated by males in an aggressive or flirtatious manner.
(3) Women who work with males find that the men close ranks, have in-jokes, and screen important matters from women by discussing them in the pub or the male toilets.
(4) A woman in a senior post often meets with evasiveness from male subordinates and, in some cases, experiences isolation from them with all matters being referred to her male colleagues in senior management.
(5) Women are 'protected' from hard decisions on the grounds that they are too 'illogical, innumerate, and intuitive'.

Walby contends that such reactions not only discriminate against women but are enormous hurdles preventing women from applying for senior management posts. She suggests that female managers and workers adopt different methods of coping with such obstacles ranging from direct confrontation to becoming 'one of the boys'. Finally, there is another obvious and prominent fact that women social workers have to contend with which is relatively absent from male experience: the threat of male physical violence. Female social workers can experience difficulties with male clients who see them as 'asking for it' if they visit them alone. We can illustrate this by referring to the experience of one of our students during her placement term. She had made several visits to the home of a separated man coping alone with three young children. On this occasion she arrived to find herself locked into the house alone with him. He had sent his children to their grandmother's so that he could be alone with her. After all, he explained, her continuing interest in him must surely be more than professional:

why did she always wear such attractive clothes and why did she visit him at home rather than invite him to the office? The incident passed off without any physical violence. Other social workers have not been so lucky. In Chapter 5 we look at the question of violence and social work in more detail. Here it is sufficient to note that there have been three murders of social workers in recent years. All three victims were women.

Women and the growth of social work

The discrimination against female workers in social work has deep roots in the history of patriarchal society and the struggle of social work to establish itself. The growing affluence of bourgeois society in the late Victorian period may not have liberated women. However, for a narrow group of middle-class women, who were either single or received help with their household responsibilities, it did liberate something precious: their time. These women sought a legitimate and socially recognised way of spending their time. The 'social' and 'personal' problems created by industrialisation provided them with a solution. Rapid, unplanned industrialisation had produced overcrowding, poor housing, high infant mortality, disease, and frictional, structural and cyclical unemployment for the working class. Undertaking 'good works' therefore benefited both groups superficially. The 'ladies' could do something worthwhile to help those less fortunate than themselves and thus gain social acceptability, whilst working-class women who were 'in need' received help, albeit loaded with a particular moral viewpoint.

One could argue that both groups were sowing the seeds of further female oppression, albeit unwittingly, by colluding with a system of help that sanctified womanly attributes as ideal for care provision and identified women as the clients needing help, rather than identifying the structural weaknesses of the social system causing problems. Furthermore, one might continue by observing that the class nature of these early forays into social work help and care reinforced the lack of identity between worker and client, undermining unity, that is feminine unity. Certainly, there was an important paradox between the female provider of care and the female recipient:

Middle class women with no direct experience of marriage

and motherhood themselves took on the task of teaching
marriage and motherhood to working class women who were
widely believed to be ignorant and lacking when it came to
the domestic task.

(Wilson 1977: 44)

The focus of practice in Victorian times was on the individual
woman and her qualities, or lack of them, rather than on the
economic, social, and cultural factors which might explain her
'inadequacy'. By glorifying motherhood and 'wifely undertakings',
early charitable pioneers condemned future practitioners to collude in oppressing women. In short, a pattern of expectations
about the female client was set up which is still evident in social
work today. Another pattern which was established in the early
days of social work development was that of women workers and
male managers. The Charity Organisation Society was chiefly
managed by men – Octavia Hill was the only female member of
its council. Today this is reflected in the fact that only 14 out of
132 Directors of Social Services are women.

A further pattern of disparity for women which emerged from
the development of the profession was the establishment of two
levels of welfare worker: those women who provided basic practical
services to clients such as Poor Law Attendants and women working in residential institutions who could be equated with the home
helps and care assistants of today, and women who had special
training and skills such as hospital almoners and psychiatric social
workers who might be likened today to CQSW holders. These
divisions have remained rife, with unqualified workers exploited
through low salary structures and lack of access to training, as
outlined in the Local Government Training Board Survey (1986).
They have to rely on their natural skills whereas 'specialist', 'qualified', and 'trained' workers enjoy better pay and career prospects.
But in the main, they are all women – often divided by their
occupational roles.

One can illustrate this further by considering briefly divisions
in entry and qualifying routes to practice. In the nineteenth century, training had to be paid for. This meant that 'social work
became hierarchically structured in such a way that the trained
elite of hospital almoners and psychiatric social workers was
almost exclusively drawn from educated women of independent
means' (Brook and Davis 1985: 10). Similarly, nowadays, the
elevated status of CQSW over CSS qualifications, and the restric-

tions on entry to CQSW courses – most are full time and require a grant to fund them – reinforce the elitism in social work.[1]

The advent of the First World War cemented women's role in providing and maintaining the helping 'backbone' of society. Mary Carpenter, Louise Twining, and Florence and Octavia Hill acted as powerful advocates of the 'moral force' of women in fighting vice and crime with education and welfare. Moreover, the position of women in civil society was enhanced by the suffragette movement and the gaining of the vote. However, it was not until the Second World War that structural and policy changes occurred to ensure the establishment of social work as a recognised profession – one deemed appropriate and even necessary for women to occupy.

The requirements of war disrupted 'normal' family life and exposed many gaps in health and welfare provision. This, in turn, gave rise to the expansion and standardisation of state provision. During the war women again proved themselves to be 'exceptional' in the field of welfare work. They set up day nurseries, staffed the probation service, organised and administered social services. With men away at war the chance existed for middle- and upper-class women to influence directly the policy and management of social work. However, greater involvement was often bought at a price. For example, like women in industry, these women found that their efforts were not considered to be worth the scale of remuneration given to men (Brook and Davis 1985: 12). Not only were their efforts in this field under-rewarded but once again they furthered female oppression: many services, for example day nurseries, which they set up and ran, were not for the good of women and children but for the war effort and were quickly forgotten in the rush to re-establish 'normal family life' after the war. Women who had been working in factories and state civil services were then expected to return to their 'natural' mothering and domestic roles. As we shall see, much of the ideology which dominated post-war welfare thinking was indeed about the 'reconstruction of normal family relations'; women were needed to spearhead the creation of what Beveridge called 'a proper domestic environment'.

Back to the family

Backed by the findings of the Curtis Committee in 1945, post-war social workers aimed to build up and support family groups. Moreover, the linchpin in family reconstruction was identified as the wife/mother. The Beveridge Report reinforced this 'business as usual' attitude to women and the family: 'The great majority of married women must be regarded as occupied on work which is vital though unpaid, without which their husbands could not do their paid work and without which the nation could not continue' (1942: 49).

Not only was the idea that women should remain faithful to their men but also they should breed to provide a continuing work-force. Beveridge again makes this plain:

> Taken as a whole the plan for social security puts a premium on marriage in place of penalising it.... In the next 30 years housewives as mothers have vital work to do in ensuring the adequate continuance of the British race.
>
> (1942: 52)

Women have been struggling with this attribution of 'housewife' and 'mother' roles ever since, supported by a welfare service which will primarily relocate support in accordance with the performance of these roles.

With the establishment of state provision, the demand for social workers grew. Ironically the very same system which provided increasing occupational appointments for 'qualified' women were mainly designed to make sure that other women remained where they belonged – at home and not in the work-place. This was reinforced by the belief that the breakdown of family life during the war years had led to a growth in child neglect. Women who were out working, albeit because the country required it, could not be caring for their children adequately. State nurseries were no substitute for a mother's care. After the war, social workers therefore needed to work with women to re-establish good standards of child care. This ideology was institutionalised by the Local Authority Children's Department Act of 1948.

Professionalism at a price

The establishment of Children's Departments was again a doubly oppressing factor for women – although not seriously so at the time. Firstly, it emphasised women's role with children: women were thought to be the right and best people to provide child care. If 'inadequate' for whatever reason, they were to be helped to learn and compensate. Secondly, and perhaps more importantly, it created 'an increase in concern over the training and status of social workers' (Dale and Foster 1986: 34). This in turn led to the development of hierarchical and bureaucratic structures to support the delivery of welfare services, the creation of managerial posts, and consequently better career prospects and salaries. Although all these things appealed to women workers, they also meant that social work became increasingly attractive as an occupation for males. What had seemed to be 'women's work' now offered a quick way to the top in a new growth profession. This was supported by the Younghusband Report of 1951, in which the need to attract men into the service was emphasised. They were seen as more reliable, and not bound by household and child-care responsibilities.

From this time until the Seebohm reorganisation in 1970, social work developed rapidly as a profession, building up not only a career structure but a body of literature and theory which provided established methods of working. Until the late 1960s the 'tool of the trade' which dominated professional practice and thinking was casework. We have already discussed aspects of received ideas embodied in casework in Chapter 1. However, it is useful to consider briefly here how the acceptance of casework as a way of working contributed to the received ideas about women embodied in social work practice. One of the leading figures in establishing and developing this approach was Florence Hollis – a good example of a woman in a professional capacity using accepted ideas about woman's duty to promote traditional and individualistic methods of practice. In developing a casework approach Hollis built on psychological theories which were focused on working in a meaningful way with individuals. However, in doing this she was often 'gender blind'. She wrote first as a theorist and second as a woman and her recommendations were often based on an assessment of individual qualities rather than social circumstances, accepting rather than analysing societal 'norms'. For example, in writing about marital conflict Hollis provides caseworkers with a six-point guide to assess whether a woman is accepting her femininity: does the woman show

(1) a pleasure in the tasks involved in making a comfortable and attractive home; (2) enjoyment and some natural skill

in caring for her children; (3) comfortable acceptance of support from her husband; (4) a preference for staying in her home rather than working if she has young children; (5) the absence of a marked need to dominate or be aggressive; (6) preference for a masculine type of man.

(Hollis 1949 quoted in Miles 1981: 14)

According to Hollis, if some of these points are missing it might help to explain marital conflict, one solution to which could be greater self-sacrifice by the woman.

Traditional casework, we would suggest, helped to cement traditional ideas of women and family life. Its major focus on the individual helped to emphasise difficulties in particular people and situations, without examining common factors – nor did it challenge ideology about women embodied in welfare principles and practice. The popularity of casework militated against 'common organisation' between workers and clients even though they were often both women. It was not until the early 1970s that a broader focus on structures and systems occurred in social work thinking.

The coming of Seebohm, however, also served women no professional favours. In specialised agencies using individual casework techniques, women could still emphasise their 'natural qualities' and develop their empathic skills, but social work in the new generic form had less use for such approaches. Social work took on a new face. It was no longer about 'helping' 'poor' and 'inadequate' people with particular problems but rather about tackling a wide range of problem situations which affected individuals in their social context. Social work became generic, rather than specialist, unified, and organised. Methods too moved away from the 'caring' casework approaches to more assertive, questioning, and radical modes of working. Such methods fitted more easily with what has been called 'the image ... of a long haired young man, recently a student, opposed to dowdy psychiatric social workers or almoners, the young Turks against the old maids' (Mayo 1977: 9). Radical social work – the new genre – was the angry young man's terrain, and women in social work floundered, victims of the destiny they had helped to create.

For a long time, since the gaining of votes for women, collective feminist movements had not been strong. Apart from individual campaigns, like that of Eleanor Rathbone for the Endowment of Motherhood, there had been little co-ordinated active female pressure. Women had worked on male terms without question for years – supporting, enforcing, and delivering policies designed to reinforce 'women's place'. However, in the early 1970s a stronger women's movement was beginning to emerge. Its inroads into social work were uneven. For one thing, feminist theory was rarely linked to methods of social work practice. Furthermore, there was a lack of women in powerful positions within the profession to open up awareness from within social work. Most radical feminist practice in and around 'social' work took place outside statutory settings.

It is certainly true that the last ten years have witnessed an increasing number of significant feminist contributions to social work education theory and practice (see Walton 1975; Wilson 1977; Brook and Davis 1985; Dale and Foster 1986; Marchant and Wearing 1986; Burden and Gottlieb 1987). However, much of this work has a stronger focus on theory than practice. Things have changed for women in social work. But the changes have not been widespread. For example, a report published by the Local Government Operational Research Unit in 1984 still showed that in local government departments:

> even when women are well represented in non manual grades (for example Social Services) the proportion of women drops off at a certain level of seniority around scales 5 and 6... Some departments are increasingly dominated by female manual workers particularly part-timers.
>
> (LGORU 1984: 5)

Many writers have argued that the growth of large-scale generic departments in response to Seebohm opened the floodgates for men to enter the profession (see Birmingham Women and Social Work Group 1981; Dale and Foster 1986; Hearn 1985; Pascall 1986). It certainly meant fewer women managers. Prior to 1970, 20 per cent of all local authority chief officer appointments were women, mainly employed in Child Care Departments; after reorganisation only 8 per cent of new Directors of Social Services posts went to women. As Brown notes:

> The male social worker is doubly blessed. If he is married his wife will be both a source of support for him in his career, by providing personal services, and will absolve him from the major part of direct child care responsibility. At the

85

same time, he will be advantaged by the fact that a large
proportion of his female competitors in the professional ranks
are handicapped by their responsibility to attend to the
needs of husband and children.

(Brown, in Marchant and Wearing 1986: 227)

Moreover, government cut-backs in the 1980s have meant less
state nursery provision, fewer jobs available, and fewer grants for
training, all of which crucially worsen opportunities for women
to enter the profession. New Right thinking with its emphasis on
the family, community care, and the female mothering role has
not helped establish women's right to full-time work. Finally, we
would suggest that many women aiming at high achievement in
society discount social work as an avenue for success. In its current, low-valued, male-dominated state it offers a fairly bleak
prospect. Those women who do now pursue a social work career
might do so because of: (a) high levels of commitment to help
others; (b) a belief in 'commonalities' (Hamner and Statham
1987) which will allow them to advance the cause of oppressed
women generally; or (c) the convenient sessional employment it
offers. Although all three reasons are valid they once again portray
women in a conforming (a and c) or separatist (b) role.

In some ways the development of social work as a professional
occupation is cyclical. Today, once again, we find ourselves in
an era where women have to re-establish their role in what should
be a profession which encourages, recognises, and establishes the
rights of women. Unfortunately, as we indicated in the last chapter, critiques of social work theory and practice have focused on
class as the main societal division which needs to be recognised
– gender has not been on the agenda. Later in this chapter,
however, we will examine the contributions of feminist thought
to this debate. Let us first examine in more detail how social
policy perpetuates received ideas about women which are translated and reinforced in practice.

Women, social policy and welfare provision

Social work involves the application and interpretation of social
policy. Recent years have produced a spate of publications on
women and social policy (see Wilson 1977, 1983; Ungerson 1985;
Dale and Foster 1986; Pascall 1986). These, and other publications

86

by feminist writers, have stressed that although the history of social work has been primarily one of women helping other women, the background social policy has consistently worked to reinforce traditional female roles:

> One way of looking at social policy would be to describe it as a set of structures created by men to shape the lives of women... Sometimes ... it seems as if policy makers simply reproduce unthinkingly traditional unquestioned views about women's role, sometimes it seems there is a conscious attempt to create such roles because they are believed to enhance social integration anew, to reinforce them and even to punish those who reject them.
>
> (Wilson 1983: 33)

Even when social policy does not talk explicitly about women, it implies and perpetuates a particular view of women's role. 'Carespeak' has crept into the vocabulary of social policy in the 1980s – policy documents bristle with references to 'informal carers', 'daycare', 'reception into care'. On the face of it, this would appear to represent the traditional qualities associated with women providing loving, dedicated services to those in need. However, as many feminist writers have pointed out the shift in social policy is more apparent than real (see in particular Finch and Groves 1983; Croft 1986). It arises out of a wish to exploit women's informal caring role as a cost-effective form of welfare administration. Policies of informal care tend to reinforce women's experience of powerlessness. They confine the energies and ambitions of women to the 'crystal of society', the home and family care.

Keep it in the family

Since its creation, the welfare state has been built around the belief that the family is crucial to social order and well-being and that the woman's role as wife and mother is vital to its survival; she provides care and support and reproduces a supply of labour. Marxist writers have also suggested that as long as women perform these roles we will never see the end of capitalist systems because the family offers support and succour which counteract exploitation and alienation. Family life makes the male worker responsible rather than militant, allows workers to be cared for without cost to the employer, and reinforces the incentive to be in regular paid work. Family life also promotes consumerism – to sustain a family you 'need' commodities, houses, cars, carry-cots, etc. It suits the interests of capital to perpetuate received ideas of the male as the breadwinner with a right to employment, and to back theories, such as Bowlby's, which emphasise the nurturing, caring aspects of women's role. Such received ideas go very deep in our culture. Pascall (1986: 3) has written that 'ideas of women's dependency are built into language use, and are operationalised by those who draw the world for us.' She suggests that the official language and categories of care often conceal and neutralise the importance of women's roles, ensuring that many key areas of female activity are represented by blanket categorisations. She cites the example of 'one-parent families' where the 'attempts to "legitimise" single mothers under the umbrella "families" also disguises the fact that such "families" are female headed' (1986: 4). She goes on to mention further examples of categories like 'the elderly' or 'the disabled'. Here the 'femaleness' of clients who represent the largest proportions of these categories is ignored as a working policy factor, and they remain hidden as a specific client group. Although social policy is explicit about the way in which the woman's role should be defined, it is also quick to cloud explicit recognition of their needs. Instead, their dependent role is constantly reinforced. For example, on official forms women are automatically classified as housewives, and not asked about their occupation; they are assessed for benefits according to their husbands' occupation and denied operations for sterilisation without their husbands' consent. Despite the fact, on average, women live longer than men, provide more direct care for their families, and, in the face of rising divorce rates, often alone, they are not seen by policy-makers as a client group in their own right. Wilson sums it up well:

> In all sorts of ways society just grinds on as though all women are still housewives and mothers and *nothing else*. The family may be 'breaking down' – it is certainly changing, as it always has – but the ideology of the traditional family is as strong as ever, and nowhere is it more crudely expressed than in the many and various provisions of the welfare state.
>
> (Wilson 1983: 41; her emphasis)

Certainly, despite the growth of radicalism and the emergence of the women's movement as a political force, basic policy thinking remains unchanged. The focus of the 1950s on 'problem families' remains. However, today it is tempered by the 'cycle of deprivation' theory from the 1970s, which sees low-income families as responsible for a lack of development in their children through bad management and upbringing. One answer to this was the introduction of Family Income Supplement – which effectively underwrites a system of low wages and reinforces the idea of the family unit. The 1965 White Paper *The Child, The Family and the Young Offender* and the 1969 *Children and Young Persons Act* sought to help delinquent children by returning them, with state support, to their families wherever possible or providing substitute family conditions. Despite growing numbers of female-headed single-parent families, housing policy has constantly militated against the lone mother, whilst the Cohabitation Rule deterred women from forming relationships which might provide them with other forms of support. As Wilson points out, 'the cohabitation ruling only embodies in a slightly more glaring form the innermost assumption of marriage which is still that a man should pay for the sexual and housekeeping services of his wife' (1980: 77).

Social Security policy has continuously assumed that a woman should depend financially upon a man if she is having any kind of ongoing relationship with him. Only the male partner could claim benefit, until 1983 when an EEC directive forced the government to use 'couples' as the unit of assessment with either partner as claimant. Although this was a move which benefited women, the resultant eligibility criteria are now so complex, demanding evidence of 'attachment to the labour market or good reason for absence from it' (Pascall 1986: 215), that women may not be able to establish their right to claim if, for example, they are full-time mothers.

The family unit remained the basic unit of social policy in the 1970s and 1980s. If anything, it witnessed a resurgence as the focus of policy considerations. For the New Right, 'society rests upon the tripod of a strong family, a voluntary church and a liberal minimum state. The family is the most important leg of this tripod' (Johnson 1982).

State benefits, women's losses

In the General Election campaign of 1987, the Labour party promised a Ministry for Women with the slogan 'Labour – Listen-

ing to Women'. It supported policies on sex equality and discrimination plus a revamped Equal Opportunities Commission, better
public transport, more nurseries, and better health screening. The
Alliance offered a 'Carers Charter' with promises of benefits for
all who care for sick, handicapped, or elderly people at home,
plus extra carers' support services and special schemes. Neither
party won the election. The Conservatives, who did, offered little
apart from an expanded system of cervical cancer screening. As
St John-Brooks (1987: 14) points out, their manifesto contained
a 'section on animal welfare, but nothing on the welfare of women.
Little attention is paid to women's special problems either at work
or as carers in the home. Yet much Conservative social policy
depends on women as unpaid carers.' We would contend that
Conservative welfare policy since the first Thatcher administration in 1979 has contributed significantly to the erosion of women's
benefits. In 1987 the universal maternity grant was abolished
despite long campaigns to have it increased. It was replaced by
a new means-tested grant available to women in receipt of Family
Income Supplement, Supplementary Benefit, or Housing Benefit
Supplement, and who had savings of less than £500. Maternity
pay was replaced by statutory maternity pay and became the
responsibility of employers, many of whom are reluctant to pay
up. What were the welfare rights of motherhood become contested
privileges. Moreover, the new administration of 1987 introduced
major social security reform in April 1988. Under the terms of
this development Family Credit will replace Family Income Supplement and will be paid through the wage packet rather than
as a benefit. New pension schemes will work against casual workers or those with low earnings from part-time work – both mea-
sures which appear to entrench the role of the male breadwinner
and undermine areas of policy where women have made some
headway.

What does this brief review of social policy tell us about the
received ideas surrounding women and the family in social work
practice? Above all, social policy hinges around images of women
as dependants of male earners; that is, they are seen as mothers,
wives, the unwaged, and as people with special nurturing qualities.
These images are reinforced by the eligibility criteria for benefits,
the limited range of support services provided, and the growing
emphasis, albeit tacit rather than 'up front', on women as the
main providers of community care. A century on from the beginnings of welfare work, despite the enormous changes that have

taken place in women's lives, women are facing similar hurdles. Resources have not changed because the old received ideas still exert a tenacious hold on social policy thinking about women and the family.

Social workers are often enforcers of social policy through practice. It is this area of practice which we want to examine in the next section. How does social work practice reinforce received ideas about women, particularly in a climate of social policy where 'patterns of living for women and their parenting behaviour are becoming more circumscribed' (Hamner and Statham 1987: 13)?

Women and social work practice

In the last section we argued that social policy is not only riddled with but based on received ideas which contribute to women's exploitation and subordination. Although there have been feminist critiques of social policy, there have not been until recently concomitant feminist critiques of social work theory and practice. Even when such critiques exist, it is difficult to establish a uniform base for action. Rather like the situation in Marxism which we examined in Chapter 2, there is no single feminist perspective which translates neatly into action. Instead there are a number of feminist perspectives which offer conflicting interpretations of current social work theory and practice. Each casts new light on the condition of women and social work, but no common solution. We will return to this point later in the chapter. It would be fair to say, therefore, that as Dale and Foster (1986) point out, social work practice has continued to develop with welfare professionals (mainly women) exercising control over clients (mainly women). This control is possible because the nuclear family and women's crucial role in it still remain the key concepts underwriting social work theory, practice, and policy-making. This is despite the arguments of many writers pointing to the decline of the nuclear family (Statham 1978; Barrett and McIntosh 1982; New and David 1985).

Female clients are often described in social work reports in terms of their prowess within the family or their child-rearing qualities; such terms as 'inadequate mother', 'depressed housewife', and 'unsupported wife' are frequently found on social work files. Social work authors have noted that getting the 'best deal' for a female client may entail emphasising her domestic situation in formal reports – especially playing up her role as 'a good mother' (Birmingham Women and Social Work Group 81; Dale and Foster 1986). They also contend that female social workers help themselves and their clients if they conform to the received idea of the good wife and mother or single woman of good standing. To be assertive in court is less successful than to 'respectfully recommend' – the language of subservience. Male clients too tend to receive less harsh treatment in the courts if they can boast support from 'a loving wife'. Such collusion reinforces stereotypes; the courts, social security offices, housing departments, and social workers all perpetuate systems which bear little semblance to reality, but which offer 'safe ground' to negotiate accepted outcomes. Social work practice also operates on received ideas about how men and women should behave. This again is reflected in reports, judgements, and recommendations for action. Hudson (1983) suggests that when social workers recommend that young delinquent girls should be taken into care on the grounds of being in 'moral danger' or 'beyond control', they are exhibiting adherence to traditional 'wisdom'. Such recommendations imply that girls who spend their time 'sexually acting out' on the street need saving from themselves or protecting from poor parenting. Hudson goes on to attest that girls who appear on 'criminal charges' tend to have their appearance and behaviour examined whereas boys do not. It is all right for boys to be engaged in street activity – it is part of growing up; girls should be at home. She goes on to comment that the stigma attached to being taken into care for being 'beyond control' is far greater than that attached to being involved in petty criminal offences. 'What needs to be contested', writes Hudson (1983: 11) 'is whether they [girls] are at risk from themselves (as may be implied by reception into care) or whether the dangers lie in the potential of male violence on the street.'

A further area of overt gender oppression occurs in residential care for the elderly. Jack (1987) argues that in such establishments elderly female residents and female employees are in the majority. Such institutions come in for heavy criticism from feminists and other writers on critical social policy, for creating a climate of dependency. Jack suggests that any such dependency does not result merely from the care experience. Rather, it exists already due to the patriarchal organisation of society.

The almost entirely female care staff of such homes are subject to this authority [patriarchal welfare authority] and

92

have neither the professional nor social status to challenge it – they are, therefore as powerless and are experiencing the same depersonalisation and instrumental relationships as are those for whom they care – the residents.

(Jack 1987: 20)

The general picture in caring work is of a service dominated by female providers and clients but which reinforces patriarchal values and gives preferential treatment to the male client. A study carried out by the Equal Opportunities Commission (1984) demonstrates that health and social service provision is consistently provided more frequently to clients who are cared for by men, and that they receive such help and care at an earlier stage in the caring process. Female carers were found to benefit more from short-term care arrangements (e.g. respite care). However, these are mainly daughters looking after elderly dependent relatives long term, who might give up altogether if strategic help is not offered! The Report (1984: 32) concludes: 'The allocation of service support reflects needs but is mediated by a set of expectations which assume that it is appropriate for women to undertake a heavier burden of care than might be expected of men.' Moreover, we submit that social workers who resort to 'playing the system' for the sake of their female clients must portray them as 'helpless' or 'not coping', in order to achieve help for them. In brief, the state system forces dependency on women; it tends to define them automatically as helpless.

This situation places feminist social workers and clients in an embattled position. The feminist who challenges welfare provision is labelled 'anti-authoritarian', 'aggressive', 'a problem maker', or 'castrating' (Wilson 1977: 41). The struggle to work from a feminist perspective within mainstream social work is daunting. It is not helped by the ambiguity of received ideas and language which feminists themselves perpetuate. What is feminist practice? What is its theoretical value base? What are its aims and methods? We shall take up these points and examine them in detail in the final section of this chapter. We now want to explore some of the stresses and tensions in women's social work practice.

Promises and contradictions

The received language of social work is rife with words that imply dependency or failure in women. For example, social workers provide 'supervision' for 'inadequate' mothers who are often described as 'manipulative' and 'demanding', and seen as 'needing help to care for their children better', or instruction in 'how to play with their children'. Spender argues that our language is saturated with male values and the marks of male power:

> The group which has the power to ordain the structure of language, thought and reality has the potential to create a world in which they are central figures, whilst those who are not of their groups are peripheral and therefore may be exploited. In the patriarchal order this potential has been realised – Males as the dominant group, have produced language, thought and reality.
>
> (Spender 1980: 143)

Spender continues by observing that women who want to challenge male-defined meanings face huge difficulties in a language which resists the attempt to encode and preserve women-centred meanings. This is certainly true of social work.

Social work method is also guilty of gender blindness. From its inception, social work has retained an emphasis on individualism, self-help, and reactive rather than proactive intervention. As we saw in Chapter 1, such traits are highly developed in casework. Moreover, as we sought to show earlier in the chapter (p.87), social policy has continuously implied that a woman's 'duty' is to marry and raise a family, and a man's is to be 'the breadwinner'.

Against this background of received ideas from theory and policy it is small wonder that modes of working with social work clients reflected similar views of women. Society has high expectations of what women can do and if something goes wrong problems are pathologised. Casework provided an adequate vehicle for examining and dealing with such problems. Biestek, Hollis, and Towle all offered sensible and plausible ways of working with individuals. However, none of them debated 'social' reasons as to why individuals need help, none of them explicitly examined the value base in society in which social work is situated. Therefore, the fact that social workers encountered more female than male clients was unimportant – they were all just people who needed help. There was no attempt to identify commonalities between problems. This might have pinpointed women as a client group in their own right. Instead, all of the emphasis was on the individual client. This individual was usually presented in abstract terms – genderless, without any racial affinities, and living in a society which has no history, no stratification system, no inequality. Marchant's (1986: 15) comment is apposite in this context: 'Until very recently gender has not been a theoretical construct in theory used in social work. This means that questions about women have been rarely asked.' Indeed, when we look at classic social work writings (Hollis 1952, 1969; Perlman 1957; Biestek 1957), we find small but telling signs of this omission. For example, they make consistent use of the male pronoun 'he' in describing both client and worker. 'Man' is the common noun in currency. Consider:

> A belief in the value of self determination does *not mean* that the case worker plays a passive role with *his* clients. He does of course sponsor changes in the client's functioning which *he* believes will enable *him* to meet *his* needs effectively.
>
> (Hollis 1969: 13; our emphasis)

Similarly, Biestek (1957: 27) observes that: 'Only as the client feels recognised as a particular individual and feels understood with his problems will he be able to enter into a helping relationship. The success of the relationship, therefore, rests on the individualisation of each client.'

Although it was the convention of the time to write in this fashion, it clouded perceptions of possible differences between male and female clients. It breeds the notions within casework of the client as a 'neutral' person, masking the special and different needs of women and men. We maintain that this 'overlooking' of gender differences has served to blur social workers' perceptions of gender inequality and reinforce through practice images of women depicted in patriarchal society – as people who are 'inadequate' and 'manipulative' and who 'act out' etc. If you do not acknowledge and tackle received ideas embodied in social frameworks then your method automatically colludes with the dominant order.

A major theoretical influence on traditional and present casework practice is psychoanalytic theory. Mitchell (1974) has sought to trace how psychoanalytic thinking, and in particular the work of Freud, offered explanations of women's oppression through sexuality. We shall examine her arguments in more detail in the final section of this chapter. However, it is necessary to mention them here, because Mitchell, whilst advocating the value of psychoanalytic practice, also recognised some drawbacks. Mitchell (1974: 229) comments that 'psychoanalytic approaches have done much to readapt discontented women to a conservative status quo, to an inferiorised psychology and to a contentment with serving and servicing men.' Other feminist authors have been still more critical (see Horney 1967; Millett 1970; Firestone 1971). They accuse Freud of 'blatant mysogyny' and point out that 'traits' which Freud describes as 'natural' to women, for example 'passivity', masochism', and 'submissiveness', are oppressive, permitting unquestioning blame of women who fail to exhibit them. Since the 1970s many feminist writers have acknowledged that the constant use of psychodynamic frameworks in social work education, training, and practice has been a major impediment to the spread of more radical approaches which emphasise sociopolitical factors in the creation of social problems.

The question of social work language and gender dependency may be further illustrated by considering the unitary approach. This approach has been heavily influenced by the sociological writings of Talcott Parsons. Parsons viewed society as a system which is analogous to a biological organism. Its normal aim is to achieve survival, and conflict or disorder is seen as the consequence of malfunctioning parts. In this context social work could be likened to sticking plaster – binding a wound until it heals. The unitary approach does not look at individuals in isolation. Rather, it sees them as interactive parts of social systems and uses a combination of casework and therapeutic and practical approaches to achieve equilibrium between the individual and the system. The aim is basically conservative: to make the individual feel at one with the world. The language is technocratic rather than therapeutic. For example, the social worker is 'the change agent', dealing with the 'client', 'action', and 'target' systems. The approach does not address the inferior position of women in society as a specific problem. The aim of practice is equilibrium and in a patriarchal society the restoration of equilibrium means reinforcing patriarchy. Similar criticisms have been levelled at family therapy (Langan 1985; Beecher 1986; Dale and Foster 1986).

However, it would be quite wrong to imply that only the more traditional approaches have mishandled or ignored questions of gender and male power. The Radical neo-Marxist approaches have been criticised for the same defects. As the Birmingham Women and Social Work Group 81 (1985: 122) put it, the radicals 'either failed to see or chose to ignore the fact that male revolutionary heroes in the privacy of their homes sometimes beat up their wives.' To some extent the radical approaches achieved the politicisation of social work methods. However, in adopting the strategies and policies of pressure groups they tended to isolate powerless and meek clients – often women.

All too often radical social workers compound traditional received ideas about how to help women by using alternative feminist solutions but not formally acknowledging their value or fighting for their legitimation. The Women's Aid movement is an example of this – an alternative response developed by women for women when the system failed them. Women's Refuges are used consistently as a referral point by social workers in social services departments, providing an instant solution which allows them to turn a blind eye to any deficiency in their own service. Female social workers often acknowledge the value of Women's Aid but feel powerless to help alter its statutory standing. If they did so, they fear it might lose its essential character. Although such services as Women's Aid and Women's Therapy Centres provide effective models of how alternative services can be run, demonstrating both power-sharing and effective use of scarce resources, they also show a way of providing welfare on the cheap. They supplement rather than supplant the main welfare system without changing the dominant societal attitudes to women or male violence towards them. They are at best a much needed and valued resource, at worst an unwitting prop to a patriarchal welfare system. Social workers in social service departments also seem to experience difficulty in liaising with Refuge staff and inhabitants. As Watson (1983: 97) observes 'they preferred to contact workers not the battered women themselves and retain professional distance.' Traditional social work training and received ideas emphasise hierarchical role structures – female social workers therefore have difficulty in linking with Refuges where no one is 'in charge'. The issue of 'battered women' is, in fact, sensitive for statutory workers, especially female ones, for they work in a system which is palpably not designed to cope with single-parent women. In a society where men are expected to be aggressive and women to be sensitive, where social workers are not backed up by the police who, in any case, are reluctant to get involved in 'domestic disputes', 'battered women' are defined as the problem, not 'violent men'. Again, as so often in this book, we are driven back to the language and its power to 'make' meaning.

Common ground, not common subject

This quick glance at some of the developments in social work method and practice has given examples of how the social work profession has marginalised the importance of women's role and position in society. Hamner and Statham (1987) suggest that women need to overcome the diversities that social work practice creates – therapist/client, provider of resources/applicant, professional worker/client, etc. – and focus on the 'commonalities' of being women. As they put it, 'once commonalities have been acknowledged, social workers are less likely to impose their own stereotypes or personal solutions onto clients' (1987: 13). If shared experience and ideas, as well as 'methods', inform the basis of practice there is a chance not only that some change can be achieved in working which is relevant to women's position in society, but that this can be practical as well as ideological. There is much to commend in this position. However, we would want to add that the focus on method and practice, although valid in many senses, can have adverse effects. Social work educators and practitioners can get hung up on academic debate about the advantages or otherwise of different approaches. To be succinct, the method used is unimportant if you do not examine the purpose that it serves. The common problem with the 'new methods' of practice occurring over the years is their presumption of a common subject. Professional language and radical rhetoric do not compensate for an unexamined reality. It is one of our propositions in this book that the 'reality' of social work is not fixed or uniform. Traditional and radical interventions in the name of 'universal need', 'the good of Man', or 'the rights of women' are bound to strike some individuals and groups as authoritarian and oppressive. Feminism in social work, which is the topic of our next section, has been liberating and will continue to be so. However, inevitably it has brought a new set of received ideas in its wake. Some of these ideas are obviously and demonstrably liberating, e.g. explanations of women's oppression which look beyond the qualities of the individual. Others have the potential to compound oppression and introduce new forms of dependency, e.g. some women find the prospect of 'liberation' terrifying.

In Chapter 2 we argued that Marxists posit the exploited class as the basis of theory and practice. Feminism also posits a common subject – oppressed women. However, like Marxism, it underestimates the internal divisions of race, class, and sexuality which nestle in this seemingly unproblematic received idea. Feminism also gives rise to its specialised language of analysis which transmits received ideas. This again can have the effect of eroding as well as establishing common ground. 'Patriarchy', 'sisterhood', 'oppression', 'chauvinism' are abstractions. They lack precision and are therefore difficult to define, operationalise, and monitor. However, these remarks need substantiation. We devote the next section to an examination of some feminist contributions to social work theory and practice.

The contribution of feminist thought

We observed in Chapter 2 that Marxism is subject to internal divisions. The same is true of feminism. The pivotal values of feminism are still emerging and the perspective remains fettered by divisions in ideology and its forms of application. One outcome of these discussions is the lack of a cohesive feminist critique of social work practice or a coherent framework to link theory to practice. However, feminist thought is crucial to an examination of social work practice, not least because it offers a theory of power rather than of the state. In contrast to Marxist perspectives, feminism offers an analysis of relationships between groups in society, where capitalism is just one of several considerations.

Early feminists were concerned with obtaining equal rights for women by gaining the right to vote. Once this was achieved their concentration shifted to achieving a better deal for mothers and establishing care facilities for the health and welfare of women and children. This approach contained no overt recognition that women's position in society should be challenged. However, it had the advantage of appealing to a broad spectrum of women who could identify with these aims, thus giving the movement a solid base. This is an asset which is often absent from today's feminist movement. As Dale and Foster comment:

> Whilst feminist consciousness is widespread among women today, this is not reflected in an active involvement in feminist politics. The interwar feminists ... had a better grasp of the need to relate to the concrete needs of ordinary women and how to campaign for specific changes that can be won.
>
> (Dale and Foster 1986: 19)

In contrast, they suggest that feminists today are more diverse in their interests and objectives. With this diversity comes a dispersal of energies and a diffusion of power.

The renaissance of the women's movement in the late 1960s and early 1970s emphasised 'sisterhood'. 'We are all one,' wrote Densmore (1969: 118) 'we are all sisters, we all work within the same constraints.' The received idea binding women together was no longer 'motherhood' but male oppression. Regardless of caste or creed women should join together to fight male domination. The movement grew in an era when the dominant ethos was fittingly one of 'love' and 'togetherness'. However, as Barker (1986) indicates this sometimes led social workers into 'the false equality trap': differences between themselves and their clients were minimised and this in turn could prove patronising and oppressive. It is important to try to establish common ground but differences need to be recognised. Barker urges that current feminist thinking should also establish 'a practice which honestly addresses differences but which creates a framework of mutual respect for what each woman is' (1986: 89). We agree. However, we also feel bound to add that the divisions that patently exist in current feminist social work dim the prospect that this mutual framework will be realised in the near future. In our view it is possible to distinguish three contrasting positions in feminist social work: liberal gradualism, radical separatism, and socialist activism. We would not claim that these are all-embracing. However, they are a useful way to synopsise many strands of thought and action. Let us take these positions one by one and examine them in more detail.

Liberal gradualism

The liberal gradualist perspective embodies what might be thought of as the 'conventional wisdom' about feminism and links most closely with the struggle and style of the early feminists. It is a position that has evolved rather than been planned and represents a manageable approach to recognising and meeting women's needs. It views incremental change as attainable within the constraints of existing societal structures. 'Use the system to beat the system' might be the motto of this approach, albeit with the proviso that reform must be applied with reasonableness and moderation. This perspective envisages the possibility of establishing feminist practice within the state structure by gradually changing things from within to achieve greater equality of opportunity for women. Liberal gradualists want reform, not revolution.

Such an approach is not rooted in theories of patriarchy and capitalism but rather in shared identification of women's problems caused by different forms of oppression. The aim is to give women more autonomy by enabling them to gain recognition in existing structures. In this it has clear links with the suffragettes' fight for equal political and economic rights. Attention is given, in particular, to seeking equal opportunities; professional advancement and pay structures for women which are equal to men, primarily through legislative, educational, and policy changes. The goals are often short term and aimed at giving women choices about how they lead their lives. Molyneux (1984) makes the useful distinction between *practical* interests (the concrete conditions of women's position by reason of their gender and power within the division of labour) and *strategic* interests (relating to the structure of patriarchy and women's subordination). Liberal gradualism concentrates on the former. It focuses on women's needs in the here and now rather than challenging or seeking the root causes of oppression. Its strength lies in campaigns and the exercise of individual power. Its approach to existing traditional theories and methods of social work is eclectic. Dominant theory and practice will be shaped to give an active acknowledgement of women's role. For example, Beecher (1986: 76) writes of family therapy, 'therapists can avoid condoning assumptions that the man is the economic provider.' She goes on to argue that family therapy, because it is inherently interested in the inter-personal and social factors which affect a person's life, provides an 'excellent basis' for building a better understanding of women's position.

The origins of this position lie in the liberalism of J.S. Mill (1869) who argued that women had been objects of subjection historically through their physical weakness and sexual value to men. Mary Wollstonecraft (1768) had emphasised previously that social status should be determined by ability not birthright; women whose powers of reasoning were equal to men's should be entitled to equal rights. Zaretsky attests that such modes of thought reflected the early opposition of the bourgeoisie to feudalism; they saw individuals as having the right 'to rise and fall within the market place through their own efforts, rather than on the basis of birth' (Zaretsky 1976: 56). In order to release and recognise their abilities women needed to compete on equal terms with men. This could be achieved through equality of access to education and employment.

The cornerstone of liberal belief is that social status should reflect merit. Liberal feminists assert that differences in ability are nothing to do with biological sex, but arise from social and cultural processes and opportunities, in particular socialisation, education, and social welfare provision. Such themes, first rehearsed by Mill and Wollstonecraft, formed the crux of feminist writing in the 1960s and early 1970s. Friedan (1965: 318) was the first of a new wave of feminist writers to identify that 'women are kept from growing to their full human capacities'. Bernard (1972) and Rossi (1972) argue strongly that biology should not be an obstacle to women's personal development. Although biology dictates that women should bear children, the provision of proper family planning services and public child care systems can alleviate this constraint. As Sayers correctly asserts:

> an individual's ability – his or her aggressiveness and competitiveness, or intelligence and spatial skills for instance – is not determined by biological sex. Any correlation between ability and sex is ... primarily the product, not of sex differences in biology but of differences in education – differences that can be remedied through appropriate change in childhood socialisation.
>
> (Sayers 1982: 176)

What women need is *real* freedom of choice (Rossi 1972). There should be no question that women can maintain equality with men given the opportunity to do so. Women need the opportunity to develop individual resources and power through education, earning capacity, and consciousness of oppression, and use them to manipulate men! Power for Rossi lies in the accumulated resources of the individual, and that individual can equally well be a woman as a man (if the opportunities are there).

Bernard (1972) reinforces these ideas, noting that although gender can contribute to an individual's power, it is talent, ability, intelligence, and personality that are all-important. What women need are vehicles to free these talents – vehicles like education, civil and legal rights which eliminate discrimination. Consequently, liberal gradualist action has focused on increasing opportunities for women to develop and compete with men on an equal footing. They have not aimed at changing overall structures which gave rise to inequalities in the first place. Such action has been incremental and targeted at gradually changing educational opportunities and curricula, altering employment legislation and practice, and promoting public provision of birth control, maternity leave, and child care services. Indeed this approach can claim many victories, for example, the establishment of the Equal Opportunities Commission, the payment of Child Benefit direct to women, legislation against discrimination in employment, and projects to combat sex discrimination in schools.

In the field of social work, liberal gradualist action has concentrated on changing the career opportunities for women in the profession. It has emphasised the belief that you need to have women in positions of power in order to promote practice which is liberating for women. Such practice involves giving female clients confidence to utilise the systems and structures which they see as dominating their lives. Hale (1983) highlights the importance of not giving female clients the impression that oppression is overwhelming and nothing can change it, and instead encouraging them to work the system. Liberal gradualist practice can help women achieve short-term goals in existing societal frameworks. The language of this approach is academic and exploratory. Workers look to the 'development of human qualities' and 'handling the world' whilst 'recognising women's rights' and attempting to build 'feminist welfare practice'. It is creative but not challenging and reinforces through discourse the received wisdom that women, if freed from certain cultural practices, can flourish in a climate of opportunity to achieve equality with men.

Critics of the approach discount it as an example of tokenism. By singling out individuals and specific targets for intervention liberal gradualists are said to bolster the status quo. Liberal gradualism pins its hopes on 'the triumph of reason' to liberate women but is unable to offer any adequate reason why, despite significant changes in legislation and educational opportunity, this has not occurred. We would suggest that this is because liberal gradualism offers no adequate theory of the causes of sexual inequality. It implies that sex discrimination is somehow accidental or inadvertent. Liberal gradualism achieves short-term successes because its aims are practical, narrow, and limited. Eisenstein (1981) contends that such forms of gradual change could prove the catalyst for long-term radical change; the more structural inequality that women uncover in this gradual process, the more they will realise the need for fundamental change.

Against this we maintain that reliance on 'individual qualities' and the definition of people who are 'vulnerable' in the system lead to piecemeal change. Offering co-workers and clients freedom of choice in a society which daily exploits and develops structural inequalities is an illusion (see Marchant and Wearing 1986). Moreover, the approach has no coherent picture of a better alternative. Pressing for full equal rights with men is all very well. However, those equal rights will be achieved in a social order which supports the domination of nature, the accumulation of nuclear weapons, chronic consumerism, etc. The liberal gradualist approach gives women no picture of a morally and economically superior society in which the daily hindrances which afflict their full development *and* the development of men will be consigned to the mists of history.

Radical separatism

Radical separatist approaches define patriarchy as the root of female oppression. Patriarchy literally means rule by the father. Barrett (1986: 16) writes 'the concept of patriarchy as presently constituted reveals a fundamental confusion, regrettably plain in discussion of it, between patriarchy as rule by the father and patriarchy as the domination of women by men.' Further divisions exist with writers like Eisenstein (1979) maintaining that patriarchy preceded capitalism and others such as McDonough and Harrison (1978) viewing patriarchy as altered and exaggerated by the process of capitalism. Schism and division might therefore be said to be characteristic of this perspective.

Generally speaking, the radical separatist perspective views 'gender' as the most important factor in understanding women's oppression – capitalism is but one variable in the debate about the source of male power. The chief premise is that male domination exists in most western societies where predominant power is held by adult men and that the oppression of women is the result.

Examination of the question of patriarchy creates further divisions in this approach incorporating a range of theses. Firestone (1971) focuses on biological differences creating sexual divisions. The fact that women bear and nurture children, she suggests, creates an imbalance in family structures which underpins all other oppressions; to overcome such an imbalance you need to eliminate this 'sex distinction'. As she puts it: 'the reproduction of the species by one sex for the benefit of both would be replaced by (at least the option of) artificial reproduction ... the tyranny of the biological family would be broken' (Firestone in Guettel 1974: 39). Such an approach may be conceptually attractive but at present offers little scope for practical action. Mitchell (1971) argues for using sex as a status category with political implications, and advocates sexual revolution to overthrow the psychological domination of patriarchy. Such a theme can also be found in the writings of Miller (1973) and Chodrow (1978) who emphasise the pursuit of psychological constructions of sexuality as the route to radical change. Psychological explanations which elucidate the difference of the female characterise radical separatist approaches and many writers celebrate, as did the early feminists, the 'distinctive traits' that biology has created for women. Firestone (1971) and Dunbar (1970) both suggest that these traits should be valued and promoted, thus providing a cornerstone for feminist revolution. Full realisation of such concepts requires separatist action either to change the world to revolve around 'women-centred values' or for women to withdraw to a world of 'female retreat'.

Many of these concepts can be found in radical feminist social work practice. They usually involve women working separately from men either individually or in groups. Attempts to change value systems can be recognised in radical moves to spotlight male violence against women. Workers seek to expose the roots of the problem and challenge people to question societal structures which perpetuate female oppression. Such action has led to the establishment of resources like Rape Crisis Centres and Women's Refuges, run by women for women, structures from which men can be excluded and where women's relationship with men is frankly viewed as oppositional. Indeed some supporters of the radical separatist perspective advocate women-only provision in all state services and the recognition of political lesbianism with a view to seeing any relationship with men as oppressive.

The appeal of separatist approaches to practice is that they are non-hierarchical and compatible with the values of 'liberation' and 'free choice'. Feminist social workers can help clients towards self-actualisation through the recognition of the exploitative effects of patriarchy and how these mould their lives. Through raising women's awareness, radical feminist practitioners release the potential for action in women clients and workers alike. However, the effects of this approach can alienate women too. Some women are unable or unwilling to view their means of support (men) as the means of their oppression. 'Old habits die hard' is a clichéd but true expression when examining the complex inheritance of female socialisation processes; radical feminists have often found themselves offering 'truths' which are unwelcome.

The language of the radical separatist approach is both positive and challenging. Workers talk of 'reinforcing women's strengths' and 'rediscovering female worth' whilst at the same time confronting 'man the oppressor' and seeking to 'alleviate women's submission to male dominance'. It is sometimes difficult to match the supportive and assertive strands of the approach and so far no mainstream social work methods have emerged. Such approaches rest uneasily in statutory settings which incorporate traditional sexist ideologies, and are more likely to be found in voluntary or community-based projects.

Critics of radical separatist approaches argue that where attempts have been made to establish forms of radical practice within existing state structures, they become incremental. To be truly radical you have to be separate. The approach has also been criticised for focusing on gender at the expense of other divisions in society, most notably class and race, which remain real and powerful alternative sources of oppression. Women may be linked by patriarchal oppression but are powerfully divided by other factors. Many social workers would attest to the oppression experienced by black working-class women from white middle-class social workers. Alternatively in our own experience of running courses for mature students with family commitments – who are often working-class women struggling through voluntary work and night school to achieve professional training – we found ostracism by their friends and relatives. These women were seen as 'deserting' their class by training to become social workers. Other critics do battle with the idea that equality is not an objective of this approach: it is seen as unattainable because gender differences are all-important. Although radical separatism offers ways forward it often promises all-or-nothing options which polarise the situation but offer no tangible way forward.

Socialist activism

This third perspective is probably the most progressive of the three; rooted in traditional Marxist analysis based on historical materialism, this approach also incorporates ideas of male privilege and female liberation.

Socialist feminists' starting point is that the capitalist mode of production cannot be analysed simply in terms of capital and labour ... *capitalist production*, the central concern of Marxism relies for its continued operation on a system of social and biological *reproduction* which takes place in the home.

(Dale and Foster 1986: 55)

Instead of presenting patriarchy and capitalism as separate issues, the dominant view in this approach is to see them as interlinked, acknowledging both the gender blindness of Marxism and the lack of a strong economic dimension to patriarchy. Whereas other Marxist and feminist approaches concentrate on the relationship of women to the labour market, socialist feminists argue that this is only one link in the chain of inequality of opportunity. The conventional family arrangement of a woman at home looking after her children and caring for her man certainly suits the demands of capitalism but what about the gender, cultural, and biological factors which also bolster this received idea? Socialist feminists attempt to provide a 'synthesis of class – and gender – analyses of women's oppression' (Marchant and Wearing 1986: 48).

Engels wrote of capitalism: 'the modern individual family is founded on the concealed slavery of the wife' (1973: 57). Here he sees the capitalist relationship between bourgeoisie and proletariat effectively translated into the marriage relationship between man and wife. Although accepted by feminists, this approach is now somewhat outdated with ample evidence that capitalists still make profits from workers who are not supported by the family structure, viz, male black mine workers in South Africa separated from their families (Dale and Foster 1986: 85). There has also been a growing theoretical recognition that female oppression is a complex issue which denies monocausal explanation. Thus, it is suggested that patriarchy combined with capitalism presents a mutually reinforcing perspective from which to examine the roots of women's powerlessness. It links biological and social systems which predate capitalism with the current demands of labour relationships (Eisenstein 1979).

The scope of this theoretical position is therefore rich. Mitchell (1974) illuminates the debate by adding dimensions from structuralist thought and psychoanalytic theory. She argues that women's situation is a product of several structures. She names four specifically: production, reproduction, sexuality, and sociali-sation. None of these factors may be viewed independently. Thus, a woman's role in 'production' (i.e. the labour force) is partially determined by the fact that natural biological 'reproduction' depends upon women bearing children. 'Sexuality' underlies relationships which in turn affect 'production' and 'reproduction'. The 'socialisation' of children creates the expectation that women should play expressive roles to service both relationship needs and the needs of the future work-force. Thus capitalism and gender structures merge to produce forms of female oppression. Mitchell (1974) also emphasises the crucial role of ideology in oppression and uses Freudian theory to explore the ideological nature of the unconscious in constructing gender differences. The unconscious shapes and transmits ideology which in turn shapes the structures which dominate our lives. Thus in socialisation processes, penis envy in girls in not envy of a physical organ but of 'what it represents in terms of male power, authority and privilege' (Leonard 1984: 51). Mitchell's approach attempts to synthesise strands of Marxist and feminist theory and is a good example of the levels of theoretical sophistication achieved in the socialist activist approach which are largely lacking in the other two perspectives we have examined. Other feminist writers (Barrett 1986; Rowbotham 1973; Eisenstein 1979) have also attempted syntheses of class and gender but none has been totally successful. Marchant and Wearing (1986) suggests that Eisenstein comes closest, using power as her analytical tool where Mitchell uses ideology; the duality of women's oppression lies in the power of capitalism and the power of men.

A further theoretical contribution to the socialist activist perspective is the application of discourse theory to feminist thought; this suggests that the ideology of oppression is translated into effect through discourse. We shall consider the contribution of discourse theory to understanding modern social work in Chapter 4. However, it is worth noting here that where Mitchell uses the ideas of Althusser and Lacan to transform psychoanalytic interpretations of ideology into language, Coward (1976) draws on the work of Foucault to demonstrate how discourse (a process of communication which both signifies and constructs social processes) can become a defining mechanism for oppression. She writes:

We should look at the conditions of existence of transformations of the definitions of sexuality in various discourses. But these transformations do not directly reflect any of these conditions, they are produced within the work of the discourse itself.

(Coward 1978: 22)

Once again, however, this perspective leads to important divisions. For example, Wilson with Weir (1986: 107) argues that discourse theory is 'promiscuous and agnostic' and offers 'no prospect of elaborating a genuinely emancipatory strategy'. Such divisions occur throughout the perspective. For example, we have seen that there is no common agreement about processes through which oppression is transmitted although there is an overall acceptance of the dual roles of class and gender. However, unlike other approaches, the socialist activist approach survives on ongoing 'healthy' debate rather than floundering through irreparable internal division.

The debate on ideology is also reflected in the practice of this approach. We have called it the socialist *activist* perspective because its common bond is action as well as ideology – collective action. Socialist feminist social work practice is about collective action based on applying theories of class conflict and patriarchy to analyse how women experience welfare services. Such approaches are prevalent both in shaping forms of policy and service delivery. Once again they are difficult to operate in statutory settings and the most successful examples can be found in community work. Mayo (1977) offers many examples of how women have worked together in groups (squatters, child-minders, mothers) not just to rectify their immediate problems but to fight to change the policies which created them. Practice therefore ranges from campaigns like the Working Women's Charter Campaign in 1970 (which challenged the economic and social relations of the capitalist system) to work with small groups of single mothers in tenement blocks to improve conditions for themselves and their children, and individual social workers changing their ways of practice. The latter change can involve, as Statham (1978: 94) notes, freeing women from 'mind forged manacles' by looking at wide ranges of intervention which do not necessarily reinforce traditional structures which oppress women. She also suggests the development of 'women-centred practice': female social workers should build on the fact that they share being a woman with the majority of their clients and use this common base both to build relationships that work and to lobby for policy changes that will change received wisdom about 'women's role' (see Hamner and Statham 1988).

Critics of this perspective point out that often the ideology is too abstract to translate into meaningful action, that although the thinking is revolutionary the action is often incremental – just like our other two perspectives. Proponents, however, argue that although 'action' may sometimes be incremental it *is* action as a means to an end, unlike the liberal gradualist approaches where action is often an end in itself. It is sometimes difficult to co-ordinate action approaches in this perspective because of differences of primacy in the theoretical debate – should action be aimed at overthrowing class divisions, gender divisions, or both at once? Practice is often a microcosm of ideological debate.

The language of the socialist activist perspective reflects the collective and political aspects of its theory. Socialist feminist workers will talk about 'enabling women to fight for their rights' through 'collective action' and 'policy change'. They also see themselves as helping female clients to 'self-determine' and 'analyse' their situation. Individual practice is geared to moving women away from self-blame and towards examining the wider aspects of the situation, which can involve careful questioning. In response to the statement, 'I can't cope with my children any more', the worker might reply, 'Is that what you feel or is that what others are telling you?' The language can also be abstract, reflecting the ideological dimension of this perspective: workers will discuss 'women's role' and 'the relations of capitalism and patriarchy'.

The strength of the socialist activist perspective is that it

> offers the best explanation of [women's oppression] to date and allows for differing emphases in different historical periods. Attempts to keep an eye on the effects of both class and patriarchy on the lives of women can yield strategies which attack women's oppression on two very important levels.
>
> (Wearing 1986: 51)

It offers the prospect of transcending the individualism induced by capitalism by building on consciousness-raising around the recognition of the effects of patriarchy. It also provides a concrete way forward which can 'challenge hierarchies as well as cuts and

110

... attempt to link together users of the services as well as providers' (Dale and Foster 1986: 176).

And so...

The three positions that we have broadly outlined here represent a growing range of ideas and practice about and for women. As we said at the beginning of this section, they do not represent the full spectrum of feminist thought, but rather a selection of theory which is illuminating. We have deliberately not included classical Marxist-feminist approaches because Marxism was fully covered in Chapter 2 and because we believe socialist feminist approaches develop and strengthen this thinking.

All three perspectives share a common understanding of women's role in society as being oppressed and seek theories and courses of action to alleviate this oppression. However, the range of ideology and approach is huge and, we would suggest, weakening to the feminist approach overall. Feminist theory provides a strong framework through which women can achieve progressive action. One of the problems, however, in developing such a framework is that women themselves are afraid of its implications. Clients and workers find it difficult to sweep away the structures of socialisation which form the cornerstones of their existence.

> What feminism has done is something very important indeed. It has laid bare the structure of the difference against which, and within which, we are fated to struggle. It has perhaps, most of all, revealed the family as a source of great ambivalence for women.
>
> (Oakley 1987: 16)

Feminism is disturbing; understanding it is difficult; acting on it is even harder. In simple terms, feminism has highlighted many sources of women's problems, but as yet has not produced a comprehensive, compelling solution.

Received ideas about feminism have not helped the cause; it is seen to be the terrain of 'lesbians' and 'militants' and not about 'ordinary women'. Feminists are described as 'loony', 'rabid', 'assertive', and 'unfeminine'. Such ideas rest uncomfortably in a profession where the most 'ladylike' qualities of women have been immortalised. Both positions represent entrenchments in received wisdom that present enormous obstacles to change.

Women who have themselves been involved in attempting to implement forms of feminist practice recognise the difficulties. Wise (1985) embarked on social work practice geared at helping women to change their lives by acting as a 'buffer' between them and the state and offering close, caring, supportive relationships. She constantly came up against anomalies; women who abused their children; men who wanted to stay at home and care for their children when their wives walked out; people who fell outside received wisdom about gender roles. Her essential compromise was to move away

> from an exclusive identification with 'women' clients as an oppressed group to an identification with those even more vulnerable and powerless. I no longer equate 'feminist' social work with 'working with women', and instead concentrate on using feminist principles to perform what I see as a morally and politically acceptable role of social policing on behalf of the most vulnerable members of society.
>
> (Wise 1985: 62)

The Birmingham Women and Social Work Group 81 also identify the difficulty of translating feminist beliefs into practice:

> Accusations are made that because we fight for women's rights we cannot make 'objective' assessments about women, particularly on how they fight their traditional role – child care and housekeeping. We face accusations (couched in good social work terms) that we are rebelling against our sexuality, acting out fantasies through women and forcing women to conform to our beliefs and values.
>
> (1985: 83)

Brook and Davis highlight difficulties experienced by female welfare workers due to the suspicion of their clients:

> consumers have proved reluctant to support campaigns to save services they dread having to encounter and find oppressive when they do. The suspicion on the consumers' part is that welfare workers, in trying to save services, are primarily interested in saving their jobs.
>
> (1985: 145)

Female social workers face a dialectic sustained by received ideas. Although they share gender definition with their female clients, they are seen as being different; they are in positions of power, they reinforce state ideology, they are the gatekeepers of resources. As we discussed earlier, becoming a social worker changes you; to be 'professional' you must often forget you are a woman. 'Good practice' does not elevate the needs of women above the overall remit to provide professional care. Hamner and Statham address this problem and contend:

> self awareness is a valued attribute of social work. Under-
> standing ourselves, our values and attitudes, the impact of
> our style of work and behaviour on others is regarded as an
> important part of our training and professional development.
> But the conscious use of self most frequently does not mean
> a conscious use of a gendered self. We think it should.
>
> (1987: 13)

Feminist theory and approaches tackle such issues. They represent a potentially powerful dimension to analysing and assessing social work practice, by providing a means for tackling explicit and implicit received ideas about women which dominate the profession. They enable 'images of a future for women that are not simply a reflection of their present position' (Wearing 1986: 53). These are all exciting developments for restructuring social work practice but ones, we suggest, which are limited.

Although feminist theory offers an alternative theory of service delivery and method, it operates itself on a system of received ideas about women – a system without commonly agreed theoretical explanations or practical operational outcomes. Bluntly, feminism is ambiguous; it means very different things to different people. To this end we would suggest that like Marxist and traditional approaches to social work feminism offers a flawed approach. In particular it assumes a unanimity on the subject – women's oppression – which does not exist. In the next chapter we push this criticism further by examining the humanist influence in social work in positing a universal subject of need and care.

4

Social work, humanism, and discourse analysis

So far we have examined conservative, Marxist, and feminist positions in social work. With the exception of the reproductive position in Marxist social work, (See Chapter 2, pp.58-63), each of these forms is deeply etched with humanist values. There are many versions of humanism and many arguments about which one is 'right'. We cannot enter into this debate here (but see Soper 1986). Rather our concern in this chapter is with the humanist influence in social work and the challenge posed to it by discourse analysis.

At the very start it must be said that the humanist influence in social work was seminal and remains very great. 'Humanity', write Brandon and Jordan (1979: 6) is 'the essential stuff of which social work is made.' Similarly, Clark with Asquith (1985: 119) comment that contemporary social work is 'profoundly humanist'. By the term 'humanism' these writers mean a philosophy based in the conviction that human beings share essential properties which define them from all other creatures. The properties in question include 'consciousness', 'reason', 'compassion', 'responsibility', and 'choice'. Humanism is primarily a philosophy of action. It maintains that human beings, in pursuit of their own willed ends, 'make their own history'. Such thought places human beings at the centre of the world. It assumes that 'we' basically have the same problems. Furthermore, it perpetuates the idea that human beings mould and fashion the world themselves in accordance with their fixed and definite self-appointed ends.

The occupational self-image of social work volunteers a strong philosophy of expert caring and responsible intervention to alleviate distress. Social workers see themselves as helpers, carers, and enablers. Indeed 'problem-solving' has currency among many

114

social workers as an acceptable definition of what they do. As Goldstein puts it, 'the human services worker has the expertise to assume the responsibility for creating the climate and opportunity for people to find solutions to the problems of living' (1981: 438).

The standard criticism of humanism is that it treats human action as the expression of innate, timeless, human properties. In other words, human action is treated in an ahistorical and asocial fashion. This is also the standard criticism of the humanist influence in social work. For example, as we saw in the last two chapters, radicals have regularly criticised traditional social workers for using key concepts such as 'acceptance', 'respect', 'trust', 'normality', 'abnormality', etc., as common and undifferentiated properties of human beings. Traditional social work is dismissed for failing to locate these properties in the immediate and concrete socio-historical context. The result, it is said, is a methodology of social work which is both imprecise and tendentious. Consider the fetish of 'real' understanding in casework and its effects on the 'helping' relationship:

> Casework focuses on understanding a client, but such understanding emphasises clients' psychodynamics and excludes serious consideration of their values or their opinion about how to solve problems. Clients sometimes report that they have never been asked by their workers how they would solve a problem; workers simply assumed that as workers they were in the best position to decide.
>
> (Rhodes 1986: 51)

Foucault and other commentators have remarked on the paradoxical nature of humanist caring. In determining the needs and rights of citizens, humanists are said to install new and extended patterns of surveillance and control which unavoidably limit the freedom of the individual. For example, acceptance of the principle that the state is responsible for caring for individuals who are in distress, demands precise delineation of the conditions in which care is approved or withheld. Individuals are required to be examined in order to ascertain if their needs are 'real' or 'false', and whether their claims on state resources are 'deserving' or 'undeserving'. Moreover, social workers must obey an officially approved protocol of behaviour in the administration of care.

Much of this is familiar stuff. Marxist and feminist accounts of social work make many of the same propositions. Indeed it might be thought that discourse analysis fits snugly with the bank of radical positions to the left of traditional social work. This assumption is baseless. About this one cannot be too emphatic. Discourse analysis accepts the substance of many of the criticisms made by Marxists and feminists. However, it rejects the idea that they have broken free of their humanist moorings. On the contrary, Marxists and feminists are seen as attacking society and social work with the express purpose of building morally superior forms of society and social work. That is, they regard presently existing conditions as repressing or perverting consciousness, reason, compassion, and choice. The remedy to this situation is to eliminate the conditions of repression so that 'our' real essence is liberated. This is evident in both the progressive and contradictory positions in Marxism. In feminism the situation is slightly more complicated. For many feminist writers, the liberation of women is the prior necessity to collective emancipation. Even so the long-term aim is the revolutionary transformation of social conditions: the 'ideology of gender roles and patriarchy must be replaced. Feminist social workers need to develop an alternative radical model of social work, one that helps them rather than perpetuates their repression' (Langan 1985: 47).

From the standpoint of discourse analysis, such thought commits the fatal error of classical humanism, i.e. it assumes that human beings really are defined by common and undifferentiated properties which can be repressed or liberated, distorted or realised, at will. In place of this it is argued that all human things are paradoxical. Our lives are suspended between the recognition of personal difference and the yearning to be close to everyone else (sameness). Suspense is indeed the primary experience of modern times. We wonder continuously what things mean, how we appear to others, what will happen next. Precisely because of this our lives are surrounded by mechanisms geared to cut down situations which are seriously menacing or suspenseful. These mechanisms, it might be said, aim to produce the veneer of order and calm in everyday life. Social work is held to be one of the most important. Others include medicine, religion, education and psychiatry.

A strong argument, in radical humanism, including radical social work, is that the execution of will with responsibility should eliminate repression and create the conditions for the free and full development of all individuals. From the perspective of dis-

116

course analysis, this argument is invalid, for it ignores that like all human things radical practice is paradoxical in nature. There are two aspects to this point and each must be distinguished carefully. In the first place, radical humanism is said to give a one-sided view of existing relations of power. For example, radical social work focuses on the repressive effects of state care at the expense of the positive effects, e.g. guaranteeing individual rights, relieving suffering, expanding people's horizons, etc. From the perspective of discourse analysis, power is a dualistic phenomenon, i.e. it is constraining and enabling, negative and positive. In the second place, and by extension, radical humanism is attacked for endorsing an over-optimistic view of relations after existing forms of oppression have been dismantled. Utopianism is identified as the condition of radical humanism. Foucault and others have described it as a dangerous philosophy. For history shows that it permits horrifying abuses of real living people in the name of intangible abstractions (the 'unborn', the 'masses', the 'underprivileged'). The freedom which radical humanism promises necessarily gives rise to new forms of oppression. Discourse theory maintains that there is no escape from the paradoxical nature of all human things and no sanctuary from the effects of the duality of power.

Discourse analysis and social work

Hitherto, we have adopted a general approach in our discussion of discourse analysis. We have argued that discourse analysis rejects the humanist idea that human beings share core, essential features. Notions of common 'consciousness', 'reason', 'compassion', 'freedom', and 'choice', it is said, are merely expressions of humanist ideology, i.e. they refer to a mythical rather than a real state of affairs. Moreover, the radical positions of Marxism and feminism in social work and elsewhere are faulted on the grounds that they reproduce the basic assumptions of orthodox humanism. In particular, they assume that, 'after all is said and done', 'we' really are all 'one', and that resolute, responsible collective action can free 'us' from 'our' chains.

In the next few sections we will attempt a more focused discussion of discourse analysis. We will concentrate upon the precise technical components of the approach rather than its general features. At this point, we want to give the reader a rough guide to the areas we will cover. We do this in order to facilitate comprehension of what is a lengthy and detailed discussion. In the first section we consider semiotics and social work. Semiotics is the study of signs. The question of the meaning in the social work relationship is, of course, central in social work practice. It is also the obsessive concern of discourse analysis. In this section we use the methods of semiotics (forerunner to discourse theory) to illustrate the ambiguity of meaning and communication which lies at the heart of much social work practice. The second section draws on the work of Lacan to make critical inroads into treatments of consciousness and unconsciousness in humanist social work. The third section introduces the concept of 'subjectless social work'. The notion is used to consider how humanist social work might be said to 'create' social problems and 'impose' solutions upon clients. This section also includes an evaluation of the crucial idea that social work discourse is a form of power which is both a resource for social work practice and a limitation upon it. The fourth section is devoted to a consideration of Foucault's concept of the disciplinary society. We examine the place of social work in this 'disciplinary' context. Throughout our discussion we seek to give examples to advance our claim that discourse analysis has real and practical applications in modern social work. However, in the last third of the chapter we focus in detail on the cases of systems theory and the social work code of ethics. In the final section we attempt to draw some general conclusions regarding the significance of discourse analysis for 'the human services worker'.

Semiotics and social work

When a caseworker diagnoses a case of wife battering as the result of a childhood complex in the client it is assumed that a precise, fixed relationship exists between the diagnosis and the facts. The same is true of radical social work. For example, when a progressive Marxist analyses a case of juvenile delinquency in terms of the client's material deprivation, it is assumed that the language of Marxist theory bears a fixed and definite relationship with reality. In both cases language is regarded as a mere tool of communication, and problem-solving is presented as strictly a technical matter. Semiotics challenges all of this. In particular it argues that language moulds meaning and cannot be regarded as a mere inert receptacle of communication. The active role which semiotics gives to language in making meaning throws doubt on the idea that problem-solving in social work is simply a question of the understanding of workers and clients and the context in which the social work relationship is situated. In addition, language, considered in its widest sense as 'communication', is a third force in the social work relationship.

We are fully aware that discourse analysis has moved on from Saussure's *Course in General Linguistics* (1974; first published 1916) which is widely regarded as the foundation of semiotics. In particular, Saussure's claim to be embarked on the road of producing a genuine science of signs is now dismissed as a hopeless ambition by exponents of discourse theory. Nevertheless, Saussure's theory remains the most appropriate starting-point in any account of discourse analysis. This is because he grasped fully the idea that meanings are structured by language, and do not pre-exist it.

Saussure argues that language must be studied as a sign system. Signs (words) consist of a *signifier* (the sound or written shape) and a *signified* (the object which the sound or written shape refers to). For example, in the English-speaking world the written shape *sun* brings to mind the object *sun*, i.e. the star round which the earth travels and which gives out heat and light. Although there are no necessary connections between signifiers and signified in a given language, important conventions in the use of signs apply. Thus, in the English-speaking world, if a person uses the written shape *moon* to refer to the object *sun* we feel compelled to correct him. The connection between signifier and signified is indeed so powerful that we allow ourselves to be lulled into the assumption that it must refer to a natural state of affairs. For Saussure nothing can be further from the truth. If the connection between the signifier *sun* and the signified *sun* is natural we would expect to encounter it in all languages. But this is plainly not the case. Different signifiers are used in French, German, Spanish, Russian, Chinese, etc., to represent the signified *sun*. The conclusion, argues Saussure, is inescapable: the relation between a sound and written shape and the object which it refers to is arbitrary.

At first sight this conclusion may seem scholastic in the pejorative sense of the term. Yet in fact Saussure's work provides an important practical framework for examining language and meaning. Three points must be made. In the first place, Saussure puts forward the proposition that the meaning of things has a structural basis in language. For example, a term from social work such as 'acceptance' or 'sectioning' has no intrinsic meaning. Meaning is not laid down from the beginning of the world. Rather the meaning of words derives from their structural position in the language system of which they are a part. For example, the meaning of 'acceptance' is not positively defined by its essence. On the contrary, it is defined relationally by virtue of its position in connection with other signs in the sign system; that is, what social workers mean by 'acceptance' derives from their received ideas of 'judgementalism', 'manipulation', 'respect', 'reciprocity', etc. A crucial methodological consequence is attached to this, and it is important to state it clearly. From the Saussurian perspective it is invalid to conduct the relationship between the social worker and the client as if it were unique and autonomous. Instead Saussure requires us to view social work as a linguistically grounded enterprise. Language, not 'man', is at the centre of things.

The second point is that Saussure recognises that the correspondence between signifier and signified is not universal. For example, in social work the sign, *contract* consists of: (1) a signifier (the sound or written shape *contract*); and (2) a signified (the object of the signifier, i.e. a statement by both the social worker and the client about the objectives, topics, and practical arrangements of contract sessions). Contracts aim to create a genuine partnership founded upon mutual trust and openness. Yet, as we have argued elsewhere, the idea of partnership is somewhat problematic (Rojek and Collins 1987). For one thing, the social worker has access to the economic and legal powers of the state, whereas the client refers to the social worker as an isolated individual with 'problems'. More pertinently for our immediate argument, the social worker approaches the contract encounter with normative expectations about negotiating problems, monitoring objectives, and the purposes of goal-setting, which the client lacks. The social worker's training and familiarity with the knowledge base on contracts makes him or her a theorist whereas the client is a non-theorist. What the signifier *contract* signifies for the social worker, then, is incomparably more complex and systematic than for the client.

The third point is that semiology holds out the prospect of a more accurate and truthful analysis of the 'real' or 'hidden' meanings which exist beneath the surface of signs. From Saussure's theory the role model of the social worker as a sort of expert code breaker can be extrapolated. If social problems are signs of conflict or disease, the social worker is a destroyer of human suffering, felling imaginary barriers and uprooting the hidden causes of painful behaviour. Of course, Saussure's claims for semiology are nonsensical unless it is assumed that semiological methods can be used to distinguish between reality and illusion, truth and falsehood. Saussure certainly believed that this was the case. As we shall see later, he has been much criticised for doing so. Discourse analysis today argues that truth and falsehood, sense and nonsense, are no longer reliable categories. Like Nietzsche, writers on discourse lament that 'truths are illusions of which one has forgotten that they *are* illusions.'[1] Such thought raises problems for social work which are of a very basic kind. To take only the most obvious point, if the legitimacy of the social worker does not rest upon truthful knowledge of real things, what does it rest upon? We shall take up this point and examine the ramifications which stem from it later in the chapter.

Consciousness and unconsciousness

Humanism addresses the conscious self. Indeed, humanist social work might be viewed as the exchange of positive consciousness between worker and client. That is to say, humanist thought and practice assume that the social worker is conscious of the purposes of the therapeutic relationship and possesses normative expectations on the effects of social intervention. By the same token, it is assumed that clients are not fully conscious of how to remedy their social problems and, in some cases, are muddled about the causes of their distress. From the humanist perspective the job of the social worker is to offer support and guidance, define problems, and provide concrete solutions for them.

Although humanist social work focuses primarily on conscious processes, it also recognises the existence of the Unconscious. Indeed psychoanalytically based models attribute an important role to unconscious processes in the individual's maladjustment. For example, Rogers (1951) maintains that human action is motivated by the quest for 'self-actualisation'. Anxiety, resentment, and helplessness, continues Rogers, are certainly related to a lack of power and a lack of material resources. However, at a deeper level they also derive from the lack of correspondence between the 'ideal self' rooted in the unconscious and the self of conscious life. The remedy, concludes Rogers, is to increase self-expression, independence, and 'positive self regard' by others. Hollis's (1969) approach to social work is also steeped in the recognition of unconscious processes. Drawing heavily on Freudian theory, she argues that the ego is continuously struggling to maintain equilibrium by fighting off unconscious fears, drives, and repressions. An important task for the social worker, she submits, is the creation of a strong ego which is able to withstand the disruptive effects of unconscious life. Humanist social work is portrayed as the gradual, progressive triumph of consciousness over the Unconscious.

From the standpoint of discourse analysis, psychoanalytically based models of social work are too parochial in their frame of reference. They recognise the division between consciousness and the Unconscious. However, they confer privileged status on the first term and treat both terms in the pair as centred in a tangible 'presence', i.e. the individual. The extraordinary step which discourse analysis takes is to depart from the notion of tangible presence. We shall take up this argument and examine it at length in the next section in which we discuss subjectless social work. Here it is enough to note that discourse analysis rejects the idea that the individual is an autonomous or unified object. Rather, following Saussure, a relational and linguistically grounded model of the individual is invoked. The individual interpenetrates with other individuals in the present and the past. Just as in language, the meaning of each sign derives from its difference in relation to other signs in the sign system.

These ideas are unconventional and they certainly challenge the established outlook of both traditional and radical social work. For example, both traditional and radical forms of social work are based in the idea that fundamental divisions exist in the 'real' world, e.g. between the individual subject and the external world of objects, internal motive and external appearance, consciousness and unconsciousness, truth and falsehood, etc. Both obey the principle that social problems have a consecutive beginning, middle, and end. Therapy is conceived of as the 'rational' 'explanation' of the orderly sequence of cause and effect which 'created' the particular problem. Discourse analysis turns this world upside-down. Jean-Luc Godard, the film-maker, once said of his own films that they certainly have a beginning, a middle, and an end, but not necessarily in that order. The same might be said of the approach of discourse analysis to social problems and therapy. Each problem or therapeutic intervention is treated as an action; each action is a sign; and each sign is a term in the sign system.

Since no reality is acknowledged outside the sign system, the actions of the psychoanalyst and the social worker must themselves be viewed as signs. Their meaning is relational, it interpenetrates with the system of signs. One of the most important implications of this is that discourse analysis is interminable. Practical considerations may require the social worker eventually to break off contact with the client. However, there is no valid end-point to analysis.

Discourse analysis is founded upon a particular view of the unconscious and we will consider it presently. At this juncture, it may be helpful to consider briefly a case study which illustrates how the principles of discourse analysis might be applied. Consider the case of a young man, J.S., who is given a life sentence for the murder of a prostitute and repeated rapes. Consider further the reports at the trial from social workers and psychiatrists which argue that J.S. is the victim of a 'sad and deprived childhood'. J.S.'s father is said to have been a violent man. At the age of five J.S. saw his father rape his mother. Subsequently the mother attempted suicide on three occasions. J.S. had an adolescent history of spending time inside assessment centres and children's homes.

This line of analysis connects violent behaviour in J.S. as an adult by recourse to the violent events of his childhood. It is frequently encountered in many forms of social work and is especially common in casework. Discourse analysis countermands all of this. It argues that it is unscrupulous to select a particular event or sequence of events from childhood as the 'origin' of behaviour later in life. Many people experience childhood traumas but they do not all become violent adults. By proceeding as if violence were centred in the 'pathological' personality, in this case J.S., society and the law create a false division between the law-breaker and the people. Ours is not a society in which the healthy can be said to judge the unhealthy, the guiltless can deal with the guilty, the whole personality can look down on the divided or fragmented personality. Rather, from the standpoint of discourse analysis we are all divided and incomplete. We are all scarred by a network of association and loss which reaches back into the deepest recesses of the Unconscious.

We stated earlier that discourse analysis is founded upon a particular view of the Unconscious. We have now reached the stage in our discussion where we must try to unpack this view. Our theme is Lacan's theory of the Unconscious. We should say at once that it is invalid to assume that Lacan's theory is endorsed by all or even some of the writers on discourse considered in this chapter. It is, perhaps, revealing that all of the writers on discourse have resisted being seen as a continuous school or movement. It is also ironic that writers who have devoted so much to undermining the familiar idea of the autonomous, free individual should set such store by the individuality of their own theories. That having been said, Lacan's theory is appropriate because it is steeped in a relational, linguistically grounded view of the Unconscious. Relationalism and linguistically grounded principles of action are common to all forms of discourse analysis.

Lacan's work amounts to a radical reconstruction of Freudian theory. He sets his critical sights on ego psychology in all of its various manifestations. By this term he means those positions which emphasise the integrity, coherence, and heroism of the post-Oedipal ego. For Lacan, the writers attached to these positions are over-impressed by Freud's discussion of the titanic mental struggle and resolution involved in the Oedipus and Electra complexes. Freud's theory does not present the adult individual as an integrated personality. On the contrary, irretrievable mental strife is the real basis of Freud's model of the mind. In developing this claim, Lacan drew heavily on Saussure's model of structural linguistics. The result is, by a wide margin of consent, an audacious new perspective on culture, and Unconscious, and the dynamics of selfhood.

The axis of Lacan's 'new view' is the so-called 'mirror phase'. At birth, says Lacan, we possess no sense of personal boundary. The infant, having no self-image and lacking powers of physical co-ordination, finds himself everywhere in the external world, and encounters the external world everywhere in himself. Relationism has free reign in this period which Lacan calls the *Imaginary*. The mirror phase begins when the infant becomes conscious of his own image in the mirror. It lasts between the ages of six and eighteen months. This is the moment, continues Lacan, of recognition. But it is also a moment of aching ambiguity. For while the child confronts himself in the mirror he also confronts what is plainly not himself, i.e. 'his' image. The individual perceives his reflection as an object, an *imagined I* in Lacan's terminology. Thus, very soon in life, the individual is riven between identifying with 'his' image and recognising that 'he' is different. This original split is regarded as having far-reaching influence upon personal development. To put it in a nutshell, Lacan sees the individual

as driven permanently to seek personal wholeness through unify-
ing relations with others. The task is doomed. For the wholeness
so ardently desired is fictional. It is, literally, an illusion. The
individual, maintains Lacan, is fated to endure powerful feelings
of absence, conflict, and incompleteness.

These feelings are not buried in the dungeon of the self. Like
Freud, Lacan emphasises the cultural significance of the Oedipus
complex in forcing compliance in society. However, unlike Freud,
he translates the Oedipus complex on to a linguistic plane. For
Lacan, the trauma is resolved by language and its effects are
relayed in society through the restless interplay of symbols.

Let us work through Lacan's propositions one by one. For the
sake of clarity we will confine our discussion to the case of the
male child. Although it should also be noted that this reflects
Lacan's prejudice for concentrating upon male experience in his
theory of personal development. The fact has tried the patience
of many of his readers and led feminists to disavow the Lacanian
project as an exercise in sexism. What does Lacan actually say
about the development of the male child? To begin with, he maintains that in the pre-Oedipal stage, the stage of the Imaginary,
the child imagines himself to be the *Desire of the Mother*. This term
carries a dual meaning in Lacan's writings. On the one hand, it
refers to the child's belief that the child *is* the mother's desire.
Like a good little structuralist the child defines his place in terms
of the differences between signs in the sign system of which he is
a part. The key difference in the relationship between the child
and the mother is that the child has a penis and the mother lacks
one. The child, Lacan says, becomes the 'penis' of the mother,
i.e. he becomes all that might satisfy the mother's 'lack'. He
'completes' the mother. The second meaning of the term the *Desire
of the Mother* is more straightforward. It parallels the orthodox
Freudian position that all male infants focus their desire on their
main source of pleasure in the external world, i.e. the mother. It
is this second meaning that we want to pursue here. The main
obstacle in the child's path is, of course, the father. The intervention of the father deprives the child of the object of his desire. It
is very important to stress that Lacan sees this intervention as a
symbolic process. The father does not have to deter the child
physically. On the contrary, the child's recognition of the father's
symbolic position as head of the household is said to be enough
to do the trick. In Lacanian terminology, the *name of the father* is
the word of the law. All of this is open to the obvious objection

that the father is not the head of every household. In many homes the mother occupies the dominant role of the main breadwinner and 'law giver'. Against this, Lacan and the Lacanians resort to the strict logic of structuralism. Individuals do not matter. What they signify does. The father may indeed not be the figure of the law in every household. But society, in its myths and propaganda, its formal and informal systems of communication (education, religion, TV, radio, cinema, film, print, etc.) overwhelmingly presents him as such. It follows that what is 'awry' in one family or network of families is not allowed to go awry in culture at large. The child who escapes his father's law in his own family cannot escape the law of the father as it is symbolised in the 'speech' and 'writing' of society.

Freud conceives of the resolution of the Oedipus complex in terms of repression. The child abandons his incestuous desires on behalf of civilisation. The sacrifice of libido is said to be the price demanded by society for order. As Freud (1979: 34) puts it, 'civilisation is built upon the renunciation of instinct'. The ideas of repression and renunciation are also prominent in Lacan's account of the Oedipal trauma. The child, says Lacan, represses the primary drive which has hitherto been the focal point of his life in the realm of the Imaginary. With this renunciation the child enters the Symbolic order. The Symbolic order is the order of language and communication. It is an order which the child experiences as a realm of emptiness. It is empty for two reasons. First of all, this order comes into being for the child after the denial of his desire for his mother. The Symbolic order is therefore haunted by the spectre of absence, i.e. by the impossibility of fulfilling the appetite of incestuous desire. In the second place, the Symbolic is empty because it consists of the endless play of language and communication. Signs never give up their secrets. Each signifier is like a bumper car which collides with an infinite number of others without coming to rest. There is no fullness in the Symbolic and no completeness.

Lacan's psychoanalytic theory therefore endorses the view of individuals as radically divided beings. Their desire leaps from an absence which they continually struggle to fill. This is also seen, in typical structuralist fashion, as the condition of language. Signs are not positively defined by their content but by their difference from other signs in the sign system. 'Presence' is an illusion which is only produced by the contrast and difference of other signs.

Methodologically speaking, Lacan's theory requires social workers to move from case to culture. It requires, in the terminology of discourse analysis, the *decentring* of the subject. Two separate points must be made. In the first place, the whole idea of dealing with the conscious self, the client's ego, is undermined. As Bird (1982: 12) remarks, 'for Lacan, the true self is the unconscious operating by and through language and irrupting into all our lives in ways which we may never control.' The second point regarding decentring is that the Lacanian position requires social work analysis to spread out laterally, from the speech and writing of the individual to the undergrowth of the Unconscious and on to the close textured links with law, art, philosophy, religion, and morality.

The question of decentring has sweeping negative implications for humanist social work. To begin with, it is condemned for its faulty scrupulousness. By focusing its attentions in the wrong place (the conscious ego) it is said to pursue the wrong lines of enquiry which lead to the wrong answers. The second negative implication is that the hallowed self-image of the humanist social worker as an expert in care, a cure maker, is spurned. Humanist social work, it is implied, is not about care. It is about administration. Consider Goldstein's words on the purposes of social work practice:

> [social work is] directed towards changing personal or shared misconceptions of reality that obstruct healthy adaptation and problem solving. The individual may be hampered by the lack of proper knowledge *or may unwittingly misunderstand himself, others, or conditions in his environment. It is possible that his reasoning is confused, resulting in personal meanings that tend to distort reality in unhelpful ways.*
>
> (Goldstein 1981: 344; our emphasis)

The assumption of exclusive social reality shared by all rational people that this statement contains is utterly rejected in discourse analysis. With it go the notions that social workers can engineer 'healthy adaptation' and conquer 'confused reasoning'. Above all what we derive from Lacan is the proposition that in humanist social work the cure is part of the illness. Values of 'respect', 'acceptance', and 'self-determination' promise wholeness and reconciliation to clients which they never deliver. The idea of an undisfigured, undeformed relationship is dismissed as a wish fulfilment of the Unconscious.

Discourse analysis does not deny that humanist social workers possess the capacity to reduce client distress. However, it limits this capacity to dealing with 'second-order' social problems: arranging gas and electricity reconnections for clients who have been cut off; ensuring that clients receive the full range of state entitlements available to them; gaining compulsory care orders to remove children from families in which they are judged to be 'at risk'; putting clients who suffer from alcohol or drug dependency in touch with addiction support groups, etc. However, social workers do not seriously connect with 'first-order' problems. These are rooted in the Unconscious and spread their tendrils through all human things via language, culture, and the law. Many social workers complain that their work regulates their clients, keeps them quiet, puts them out of sight, and pacifies them, rather than helping them. From the standpoint of discourse analysis they are right to do so. State social work is a monument to sterile pragmatism. To paraphrase the words of Barr (1974: 530), discourse analysis regards social work as 'a process in which one patient (the social worker) cures the other patient (the client) by imposing on him his own symptoms'.

Subjectless social work

Discourse analysis rejects the *developmental* view of humanist social work which portrays 'pathologies' and 'symptoms' as developing in an unbroken chain of cause and effect towards an assigned end or point of origin. As we have seen, it maintains that it is invalid to attribute 'beginnings' or 'ends' to therapy and diagnosis. Instead it endorses a *genealogical* view which explores the clients' problems laterally as part of the structure of the Unconscious and its handmaiden, language.

The term 'genealogy' is associated with Foucault. He defines it as 'a form of history which accounts for the constitution of knowledges, discourses, domains of objects, etc, without having to refer to a subject' (Foucault 1980: 117). This is a radical departure from conventional accounts of history and action which are always centred on a subject. For example, there are many accounts of the emergence of social work and its development and practice in the present day. They treat social work as if it were indeed a unified subject which is 'born', 'grows', has 'needs', 'desires', 'aims', and 'takes' action, etc., just as if it were a living person.

128

In contrast the genealogical view posits social work, not as a point of origin, a tangible reality, but as the accessory of a complex, moving mosaic of writing, speech, and action. Consider the value of confidentiality in social work. This is prominent in most lists of key professional values in social work. However, it has ambiguities and it did not spring into the world of social work fully grown. The ambiguities do not concern us here, although it is worth noting in passing that absolute confidentiality between worker and client, in the sense of conveying no information whatsoever without the client's prior consent, is often incompatible with the organisational dynamics of large bureaucratic agencies. At this juncture we want to refer to the value of confidentiality to amplify the proposition that social work is an accessory of a complex moving mosaic of writing, speech, and action. The notion of confidentiality in social work is bound up with issues of privacy and rights. Confidentiality, privacy, and rights are interwoven with a complicated series of debates and initiatives in theology, ethics, the law, social science, public health, medicine, etc. Within this series, representations of 'man', his 'needs', 'capacities', 'wants', and 'rights' can be traced and unravelled. One can examine the entanglements between the concept of rights in the law and the concept of privacy in medicine. However, it is very tricky indeed to claim a point of origin for this series, a place in time and space where these entanglements begin. For as soon as one point of origin is 'found', prior links are 'discovered'. In this sense the subject of 'confidentiality' has no origin and therefore no unified history. Rather than speaking of linear causality it is necessary to speak of lateral linkages. Instead of history, it is structure which should obsess us. For the structure of speech, writing, and action influences what can be said, written, and done. In other words, there is a framework in social life, so familiar to us that we are barely conscious of it, so insistent that we cannot choose to avoid or reject its rules, which makes it possible or impossible to speak about a particular issue or object. This framework is discourse. Writing of social work discourse, Philp comments that,

> the discourse is a regime of truth which operates through a
> set of rules or organising principles which exist over and
> above the statement and the *oeuvre* in which it is found ...
> It is these that link together dispersed objects (from the
> aged to the delinquent); which provide the basis for diverse

operations (from care orders to encounter groups, from adoptions to welfare rights); which underlie all its concepts (from ego syntonic to alienation); and which provide for all its theoretical and practical options (from radicalism to conservatism, from repression to conscientization).

(Philp 1979: 87-8)

The concept of discourse raises important questions of legitimacy in social work, and the status of truth and falsehood in diagnosis and therapy. We will come to them in due course. However, before reaching that point we want to explore the notion of subjectless social work from a slightly different angle. From Foucault we have taken the notion of genealogy. We have argued that the configuration of knowledge, power, and expertise which social workers use is not centred on a self-contained, unified subject. This knowledge, power, and expertise interweaves with the complex, moving mosaic of speech, writing, and action relating to 'man', his 'needs', 'wants', 'capacities', etc. Derrida's work can be used to draw parallel conclusions, although the methodology he uses is more explicitly grounded in linguistics.

Derrida accepts the Saussurian principle that in communication the signifier always signifies more than the signified. For example, in social work the word 'help' (signifier) signifies (means/indicates) more than mere assistance to the client (signified). Thus, it signifies the duty of the social worker to provide help; the recognition of the state that citizens have needs; the conditions in which relief may be administered or withheld, etc. However, Derrida takes this line of thought much further with his notion of *différance*. Derrida coined this term with a special purpose in mind. In French, the 'a' in *différance* is unheard; the word registers as *différence*. The undetected 'a' is revealed only in writing. *Différance* is thus a condensed way of showing the hidden depths involved in each subject/object relationship. Derrida maintains that three signifieds coexist in the signifier *différance*. These are: (1) 'difference' the idea that one thing is different from another thing; (2) *differe* (Latin) to disperse, disseminate, scatter; (3) 'deferment', that is to put off, delay, or postpone. According to Derrida language works through *différance*. Let us take an example from social work to illustrate this proposition. In Chapter 2 where we looked at Marxist social work, we argued that collective organisation is a standard demand of radical thought. Collective organisation is obviously very different from isolated individual practice. Indeed, for most radical social workers it is the exact opposite of isolated individual practice. Moreover, the goal of collective organisation clearly requires social workers to disseminate ideas, to promote unionisation, to raise consciousness. Finally, the concept of collective organisation also carries with it the notion of deferring or postponing forms of individual practice which are out of line with collective will. In the *presence* of the concept of collective organisation, Derrida might say, we find the *trace* of *absent* signifieds. It follows that we cannot write or speak of collective organisation without invoking, albeit at an unconscious or subconscious level, different (isolated social work practice) or deferred (authoritarianism) meanings. The subject of 'collective organisation' is therefore not a centred or unified entity at all. On the contrary, its meaning derives from its place in the sign system and the different and deferred meanings which can be traced to it.

We said earlier that the concept of discourse raises several important questions for social workers. We have now reached a stage in our discussion where it is necessary to investigate these questions. Four points must be made.

First, discourse analysis emphasises the conditional, changeable character of social work. It shows that there is nothing fundamental or inevitable about the form of social work. Social work is just that: a form. Like human nature and society, it is moulded by a great many distinct influences. These influences develop certain human capacities and retard others. Like all human forms, social work can be changed. However, in common with all exercises of power, change must be understood as a dualistic phenomenon: the pursuit of intended goals produces unintended effects, it is both enabling and constraining.

Second, discourse analysis reverses the accepted priority of need in humanist social work. Humanist social work portrays the social worker as the servant of needs which spread out from the client (the subject). We have referred to these needs on several occasions in this book. Among the most prominent are the needs for compassion, respect, dignity, and trust. Social work, the humanists say, is about fulfilling these needs through the provision of care with responsibility. Yet, from the perspective of discourse analysis, this puts the cart before the horse. Compassion, respect, dignity, etc., do not arise spontaneously from the client. Rather they are constructed through discourse and the client is required to fit in with them. Need, and reaction to need, are therefore seen as linguistically grounded. As Lacan (1977: 65) observes, 'it is the

131

world of words that creates the world of things.'

Third, discourse analysis is iconoclastic. It calls into question not only the meaning of social work knowledge but even the possibility of such knowledge. We noted earlier that Saussure has been much criticised for arguing that semiology is in a position to decode myth and function as the real science of signs by exposing true meanings. The criticism turns on the argument that it is invalid to claim that semiotics has privileged status as a signified which is above the 'corrupting' influence of genealogy and *différance*. As Derrida (1981: 20) puts it: 'From the moment that one questions the possibility of such a transcendental signified, and that one recognises that every signified is also in the position of a signifier, the distinction between signified and signifier becomes problematical at its root.' There is no privileged or objective meaning because there is no privileged or objective knowledge. It follows that humanist social work is doubly damned. To begin with, it is said to base itself in a sphere of 'reality' which does not exist, i.e. 'common human needs' (see Towle 1965). In the second place, its claim that social work knowledge is more detached, objective, and truthful than other forms of knowledge is rejected as indefensible. The social worker is trapped in the restless play of language and other sign systems as are all other people. There is no escape.

Fourth, discourse analysis requires us to explore social work relations as relations of power. The purpose of social work, it is said, is to *reform* the client. It aims to *normalise* social relations by rooting out 'deviance', 'antagonism', and 'pathology'. Yet as Foucault (1975) points out in the context of the actions of the state penal system on the criminal, reform and normalisation have never been achieved. Criminals still exist; clients in need still exist. The state penal system and state social work have been monotonously unsuccessful. The question then is, why have they survived? For Foucault, and other writers on discourse, the answer is that they have been spectacularly successful in achieving another latent goal of the system: the deliberate production of the pathologised personality. The prison and welfare services are said to have created the delinquent and the client by specifying the nature of pathology and abnormality and ruthlessly hunting down anybody who falls into the determined categories. From the perspective of discourse analysis then, the social work discourse (a) *creates abnormality*, by specifying the nature of the pathological; and (b) *imposes solutions* on the client by its access to the institutions of discipline, punishment, and moral regulation.

However, these are controversial and contentious points. In order to defend them it is necessary to go much deeper into the treatment of discipline and power in discourse analysis. This task will occupy us in the whole of the next section of our discussion.

Social work and the disciplinary society

Foucault uses the term 'disciplinary society' to characterise modern social conditions. However, it is necessary to use the term with care since the meaning which Foucault attributes to it is very specialised. In everyday language the term 'discipline' means the use of power to alter conduct in predetermined ways. The term presupposes an inequality of power between the person who *disciplines* and the person who is *disciplined*, e.g. a mother might be said to discipline her child, an employer disciplines a worker, a court disciplines an offender. Generally, social workers resist the suggestion that occupational practice is associated with disciplinarianism. The professional self-image is, as we have already had occasion to note, of a helper, a carer, and an enabler. Moreover, the development of problem-centred approaches, task-centred models, and contract work reflects a self-conscious consumerist movement in social work which seeks to 'bring in the client'. Despite all of this the social work relationship is quite clearly a relationship of inequality. For one thing the social worker has access to the economic and physical powers of the state which the client lacks. Furthermore, the knowledge of the social worker regarding the dynamics of caring and helping relationships tends to be more systematic and rigorous than that of the client. Still, it would be wrong to deduce from this that the social worker is basically free to exercise power over the client at will. On the contrary, as Philp (1979: 90) affirms, 'the social worker operates in the control of discourse.' That is, action and reaction in social work, insight and blindness, are rule-bound. The social worker disciplines and is disciplined. In part this is a consequence of the specialised training that social workers receive. State certification in social work requires the student to learn to speak and write in officially approved ways, that is to speak and write in the discourse of social work. As one commentator remarks:

It is this [familiarity and ease with social work discourse] which is being taught, examined and certificated, not what

133

> It is this [familiarity and ease with social work discourse] which is being taught, examined and certificated, not what you personally think or believe, though what is thinkable will of course be constrained by language itself ... Those employed to teach you this form of discourse will remember whether or not you were able to speak it proficiently long after they have forgotten what you said.[2]

The discourse of social work acquiesces unreflectively in the conventional systems of western rationality which impose order on the world through the order of words (normal/abnormal, healthy/ ill, right/wrong). It therefore participates in the continuous renewal of existing arrangements of power and domination. But this is only half the matter. Social work discourse conforms to a particular regime of discipline and punishment regarding the offender and the pathological personality. In order to comprehend the mechanics of the social work discourse it is necessary to produce a genealogical investigation of this regime. This is not an easy task. Foucault's analysis of the genealogy of power and discipline is very complicated. His analysis is discontinuous and his style is frequently elliptical and allusive. Moreover, the whole method of discourse analysis cries out to beware of accounts of social processes which purport to show that they consist of a consecutive beginning, middle, and end. We will break with this methodological principle in what follows. We will do so because we need to convey the basic features of Foucault's genealogical view in an abbreviated form. We judge that this requirement for this book overrides distinctions of methodological propriety. We shall make our case in summary form, five points in all, beginning with the great transformation in discipline and punishment, from spectacle to surveillance.

(1) The rituals of state punishment used to focus on torture as a public spectacle. The gruesome public torture of the regicide Damiens on 2 March 1757 is used by Foucault as a case in point. The convicted man's flesh was torn by pincers, molten lead, boiling oil, burning resin, wax, and sulphur melted together and poured into the wounds. He was then drawn and quartered by four horses and his body burnt to ashes. Damiens's case is extreme, but it nonetheless illustrates the general principle of penal repression that existed at this time. Punishment was centred on the body, and the purpose of

134

punishment was twofold: deterrence, and the symbolic affirmation of collective sentiments of 'right' against the wrongdoer, e.g. in the public execution it appears as if society as one participates in the torture and dispatch of the condemned person.

(2) The spectacle of public execution has been replaced by a new system of discipline and punishment which aims to regulate conduct by surveillance and prevention. As Foucault observes,

> in the early nineteenth century people appear who make it their business to involve themselves in other people's lives, health, nutrition, housing; then out of this confused set of functions there emerge certain personages, institutions, forms of knowledge: public hygiene inspectors, social workers, psychologists.
>
> (Foucault 1980: 2)

(3) The new system of discipline and punishment focuses on the mind, not the body. Instead of concerning itself with the question of criminal responsibility for law-breaking it is more concerned with explaining the causality of crime by relating it to the client's biology, history, psychology, etc. Donzelot (1979) suggests that a new realm of consideration is opened up to discourse. 'The social' is neither public not private. It is a realm in which the balance of power rests with the social worker, the psychiatrist, the juvenile court, etc. It is the most intimate and minute details of a person's life that are opened up to professional scrutiny and weighed on the scales of justice.

(4) What caused the new system? Genealogically speaking, there was no single cause. The humanist discourse on the wants, needs, and capacities of man played their part. New mechanisms of penal control were also instrumental. Foucault cites Bentham's design for a *panopticon* as an example of the new technical breakthroughs. The panopticon was a circular prison with cells around a central observation point which offered continuous surveillance of the prisoners. However, there was also the fear of the labouring class which became an obsessive preoccupation among the ruling class in Europe after the French Revolution. Illegality and protest which hitherto had been seen as merely dangerous were now perceived as taking a political turn.

(5) What are the purposes of the new system? The 'creation' of the delinquent and the discourse surrounding pathological behaviour personalised illegality. It robbed protest and reaction of their populist and 'revolutionary' dimensions. Moreover, the new system scrupulously avoided creating martyrs by torture and execution. Rather, it sought to defuse aggression and alienation by instruction, observation, measurement, drill, and routine. Rehabilitation replaced repression as the guiding principle of the system. With the creation of 'the social', power filtered down from the penal apparatus to the 'scientists' of care, help, and adjustment. In the nineteenth century, and especially in the following decades, Foucault (1975: 306) argues, 'medicine, psychology, education, public assistance, "social work" assume an ever greater share of the powers of supervision and assessment.' The new system aims to perpetuate order and control through care and self-discipline. Illegal and deviant conduct is 'explained' in terms of personal pathology. The remedy lies in acceptance, training and consciousness-raising. The new 'remissive' culture[3] aims to traverse all points and normalise behaviour. Social work plays a leading role in the process of normalisation. Foucault again:

We are in the society of the teacher-judge, the doctor-judge, the educator-judge, the 'social worker'-judge; it is on them that the universal reign of the normative is based; and each individual, wherever he may find himself, subjects to it his body, his gestures, his behaviour, his aptitudes, his achievements.

(Foucault 1975: 304)

In the disciplinary society, few are born into normal existence, most have it thrust upon them. The family, education, the law, religion, and the vast array of helping and caring professions coax and guide, train and cajole, the individual into acting in officially approved ways, even to the point of putting him behind bars to teach him his lesson.

Discourse care and control: a summary

At this point in our discussion it may be helpful to summarise

136

our main propositions on discourse analysis and social work. We have argued that discourse analysis produces a linguistically grounded model of social work. It submits that there are no fixed or original meanings in social work. What a term signifies is defined negatively by its differences from other terms in the sign system. Key terms in social work such as 'need', 'client welfare', 'respect', 'acceptance', 'confidentiality', and 'consciousness-raising' do not reveal the 'real' world, they merely assemble it. The Unconscious plays a full part in this process. Ambiguity, condensation, and distortion abound in diagnosis and therapy. Developmental models of pathology and helping which proceed through linear analysis must be replaced by structural models which proceed through lateral analysis. The sign must be followed through the chain of links and differences with other signs in the sign system, rather than through a quest to find its source. Classification (of clients, problems, duties, etc.) is at the heart of social work discourse; and classification means control. The various approaches to social work practice – psychodynamics, task-centred work, the varieties of Marxism and feminism – each define the client and require him to live up to the classification of his symptoms and latent capacities. The client is required to fit in with the classification rather than the other way round: 'the social worker creates a subject who is characterised by a universal subjectivity, one which applies to all individuals and yet no one in particular' (Philp 1979: 91). The subject is subjectless. However, the attempts to measure and observe, to differentiate and classify, exert a profound disciplinary effect. Social work is not about care, it is about discipline.

These are contentious and controversial propositions. We have tried to back them up with examples throughout our discussion. Even so there is room for attempting a more detailed consideration. This we propose to do in the next two sections by using the systems approach and the Social Work Code of Ethics as case studies.

The systems approach

The systems approach arose in reaction to casework, group work, and community organisation. Pincus and Minahan (1973, 1977), the writers who are generally acknowledged to be the main architects of systems theory, do not mince words in speaking up for what the theory signifies. Systems theory, they argue, 'represents a reformulation of the base of social work practice which gives social work a clear place among the human service professions' (Pincus and Minahan 1977: 104). What is the basis of this 'reformulation'?

Systems theory does not begin with the isolated individual, the person in distress. Not does it begin with the social system which is said to mould individual conduct in distinctive ways. Rather it begins with the *interaction* between the individual and social *systems*. The plural form is vital. Methodologically speaking, systems theory recognises three kinds of resource system which the client is keyed into. These are: (a) informal resource systems e.g. family, friends, neighbours, co-workers; (b) formal resource systems, i.e. the network of interest groups in society such as trade unions, professional associations, neighbourhood groups, etc.; (c) societal resource systems, i.e. the welfare agencies of civil society such as schools, hospitals, housing authorities, consumer advice organisations, etc. In the normal run of things, Pincus and Minahan maintain, these systems work in harmony to enable the individual to match personal aspiration to achievement. However, it is very important to note that these systems are very complex. From time to time, mismatch and conflict will occur. This is where the social worker comes in. Pincus and Minahan appear to regard the social worker as a cross between a servant of client need and a social mechanic. They (1973: 15) list seven major functions of social work:

(1) Help people to develop their problem-solving and coping capacities.
(2) Build bridges between people and resource systems.
(3) Facilitate the interaction between people and resource systems.
(4) Facilitate interaction with resource systems.
(5) Participate in the development and modification of social policy.
(6) Appraise clients of state entitlements.
(7) Act as an agent of social control.

According to Pincus and Minahan one of the most important mechanisms of social work is the working agreement. Working agreements are said to establish a clear framework for the work relationship. They may be written or verbal in form. However, they always specify three things: (a) the main goals of the work relationship; (b) key tasks to be performed by each party in pursuit of the mutually agreed goals; (c) the basic means of goal achievement. Part of the process of negotiating a working agreement is to identify the *client system*. This consists of the formal and informal resources network that surrounds the client, e.g. the family, friendship relations, work/leisure groups, and the organisation which employs the social worker. The identification of the client system helps the social worker to situate the client and enables both worker and client to determine realistic goals and means in the working agreement. Another major feature in negotiating working agreements is identifying the *target system*. This refers to 'those people the change agent needs to influence in order to accomplish the goals of his change effort' (Pincus and Minahan 1977: 82). The change system, the client system, and the target system are said to be useful labels to mark the main components of the social work territory. However, social work only comes to life when these systems interact in motion. Pincus and Minahan (1973: 63) use the term *action system* to refer to the generic motion of the three systems meshing together.

Routine objections to systems theory are that it is ahistorical: it tacitly endorses the existing distribution of power and inequality in society by assuming it to be 'natural' or 'inevitable'; it regards conflict and dissent as temporary maladjustments in social systems as opposed to continuous features of interaction; it tends to regard conflict as a negative phenomenon which threatens the inveterate harmony and balance of the social system.

We have listed these critical points briefly because our main concern in this section is to examine the criticisms that flow from the perspective of discourse analysis on systems theory. We shall make three points.

The first point is that systems theory may be attacked for reproducing the central defect of humanism; that is, it assumes that a fixed and definite relation exists between language and meaning, and that language merely reflects reality. Against this, as we have seen, discourse analysis argues that language constructs the world. Subject and pathology, meaning and action, spring from the order of social work discourse. They do not exist 'in reality'.

The second point is that systems theory addresses the conscious, centred subject. True, it allows for Unconscious motives, desires, forces of repression, and resistance. Yet the primary task of therapy is to work with the conscious self to build action systems which will restore 'normality' to the 'damaged' or 'disturbed' personality.

We have argued that discourse analysis is highly critical of forms of social work which focus on the conscious ego. Discourse analysis submits that the Unconscious breaks through into all aspects of social life. Our desire, practice, and very language are marked indelibly by the Unconscious. In neglecting this fact, systems theory, which claims to be the most hard-headed and realistic of all approaches to social work, is dismissed as the most naïve and self-deluding of approaches.

The third point is that the systems approach is centred on the concept of the social system. Helping consists of building working agreements which establish the objectives of practice (method goals) to effect a realignment between the subject (the client) and the object (the social system). However, from the perspective of discourse analysis, the idea of the social system as a tangible presence is a delusion. As soon as one tries to specify the boundaries of the system one finds oneself making arbitrary decisions and judgements, i.e. one decides and judges by fiat. The concept of the social system is a *metaphor*. The further we descend into its imagined depths the more we find ourselves talking about talk and writing about words, i.e. discovering discourse.

The social work code of ethics

Codes of ethics have been published on both sides of the Atlantic (BASW 1975; NASW 1980). Basically they are exercises in foundationalism. That is, they aim to distil the ethical principles of social work into a guide for practice. The codes specify the values and responsibilities of professional social work. Although the two codes were formulated in different countries by staff representing different occupational cultures and traditions, there is substantial common ground between them. For example, both define ethical principles in individualistic rather than collectivistic terms. In the words of the BASW code:

> Basic to the profession of social work is the recognition of the value and dignity of every human being, irrespective of origin, status, sex, sexual orientation, age, belief or contribution to society. The profession accepts a responsibility to encourage and facilitate the self-realisation of the individual person with due regard to the interests of others.
>
> (BASW 1975: 2)

The self-realisation of the individual requires strong commitment from the social worker. For example, the NASW code calls upon the social worker to serve the client with 'devotion, loyalty and determination' (1980: II.F.I). The social worker is encouraged to participate in what Fox (1974) calls 'high trust' work relations with the client, that is relations in which the client is treated as a capable social actor with the capacity for self-understanding and making sense of external events. The corollary of high trust relations is the recognition of the client's right to privacy and the confidentiality of exchanges in the social work relationship. However, the values of trust, confidentiality, and respect are tempered, in both codes, by the powerful endorsement of professionalism. Caring and helping are administered on professional principles of detached assessment and objective resource management. Both codes encourage the social worker to get close to the client; but not too close. In other words, there is a strong requirement of restraint in social work practice, and it is urged on behalf of society. Both codes, in fact, demand dual loyalty from the social worker: to serve the client and to serve the welfare of society. Critics have seized upon this dualism to argue that each code is self-contradictory (Clark with Asquith 1985; Rhodes 1986). The interests of the client and the interests of society, it is said, are often in conflict. There is little that the social worker can do to reconcile them.

A similar line of criticism opens up from discourse analysis. However, whereas most critics of the code develop their attack in order to retrieve the notion of clear and serviceable ethical principles in social work, discourse analysis rejects the notion outright. Foundationalism in human affairs is condemned as a dead-end because it implies that language and ethical principles can be treated as fixed and static things. Such an implication ignores the equivocal status of language, communication, and therefore principles of behaviour: communication is multidimensional, meanings change, principles become prisons. The idea of foundationalism in social work and elsewhere is further attacked from another angle, for it is said to threaten to produce standardised ways of seeing and forms of practice which will suppress individual difference. Social work thought and practice will be evaluated according to their curve of deviation from the accepted margin. The result would be the magnification and intensification of authoritarian tendencies in social work.

Foundationalism also reproduces uncritically the humanist idea that knowledge and practice can be centred on a subject. The codes are designed as guides which set out officially approved principles of intervention and practice. These principles are centred on a subject (the social worker) and designed to activate change in an object (the client or society). At first sight this seems a sensible and unobjectionable way of proceeding. However, if one digs deeper into the principles of intervention and practice things no longer look so simple. Consider the main principle of social work which is endorsed in both codes, that ethical values relate to the value and dignity of every human being. Earlier we referred to this as the 'individualistic' character of both codes. Individualism is based in the idea of the person. 'The person' is certainly a familiar concept. However, to claim or suggest that merely because it is familiar it can be applied unproblematically is to confuse familiarity with accuracy. As we have seen, discourse analysis maintains that conventional ways of thinking, speaking, and writing are marred because they are predicated in the idea of a conscious subject, and therefore marginalise the place of the Unconscious in everyday life. The notion of 'the person' involves a similar error. Two points must be made. In the first place, it ignores the theoretical point that the person cannot be said to exist 'naturally' or 'spontaneously'. Rather, the idea of 'the person' is said to be an aspect of discourse. Individuals are required to fit in with the concept of what 'the person' signifies. The second point is that the concept of 'the person' raises all sorts of immediate and concrete questions of a practical nature regarding social work practice:

> is it often not clear exactly what a 'person' is. Where does a person end, and environmental influences begin? What aspect of the person is to be respected, when one is assuming that much of their thought and behaviour is deeply influenced by factors of which they may not even be aware?
>
> (Dorwick 1983: 14)

From the standpoint of discourse analysis, these objections fuse to make the two codes improvident in theory and inoperable in practice.

Conclusion: *doxa* and deconstruction

If discourse analysis is critical of humanist social work on the

grounds that it is improvident and inoperable, it nonetheless re-
frains from writing off the humanist tradition as meaningless. On
the contrary, humanism is recognised as the dominant frame work
of power in society. Discourse analysis tirelessly opposes this
framework because it is said to confuse domination with freedom,
indoctrination with common sense, and history with nature. The
term *doxa* is used in discourse analysis to refer to 'the prevailing
view of things, which very often prevails to the extent that people
are unaware it is only one of several possible alternative views'
(Sturrock 1979: 54). We have argued that the *doxa* of social work
is humanism. Moreover, we have indicated that its main features
are: individualism; the view that language simply reflects reality;
the problem-solving approach to social problems which seeks to
account for them in a final or definitive way; and the centring of
resources on the conscious subject.

Discourse analysis is concerned, among other things, with
unravelling the veil of *doxa* and awaking the sleeper from sleep.
So potent is this concern that discourse analysis is occasionally
referred to as 'deconstructive criticism'. By this is meant a subver-
sive approach which calls into question received ideas of language,
truth, reality, history, interpretation, and forms of critical understanding. It is only too easy to deduce from this that *all* meaning
is ideological and that every action is doomed to sink into the
empty chasm of signs. However, this would be to mistake criticism
for negativity and thus give a one-sided account of discourse
analysis. In fact the *doxa* which discourse analysis attempts to
deconstruct is quite specific and the process of deconstruction has
tangible aims.

The *doxa* is humanism which treats 'man' as the possessor of
universal, undifferentiated desires, needs, and capacities. Traditional social work is therefore criticised for being ideological and
unrealistic. It is said to be ideological because it maintains that
the individual client (the conscious subject) is at the centre of
social work practice, and moreover that the goal of social work
is to engineer equilibrium between the client (the subject) and
society (the object). Traditional social work is said to be unrealistic
because it underestimates the role of social work discourse in
'creating' problems and 'imposing' solutions. Thus the discourse
of social work produces a 'universal subjectivity' which applies
to 'all individuals' yet 'to no one in particular'.

Radical social work is antagonistic to traditional social work.
However, from the standpoint of discourse analysis, it is situated

on the same plain of humanist *doxa* and thus commits the same errors. For example, Marxism posits an oppressed class which through its own actions is destined to overthrow capitalism, the engine of all its miseries, and build a new society. In this new society the capacities of the individual can flourish and the desires and wants of the individual will be answered. Feminism takes a similar turn in its call for the women's movement to wage a collective assault on patriarchy. In both cases it is assumed that language corresponds with reality, that collective action can be based on collective need or desire, and that problem-solving is capable of producing fixed and definite solutions. On each count discourse analysis rejects the radical position as a delusion. Thus, language is said to construct 'reality' rather than to 'reflect' it; collective need or desire is said to be an effect of discourse, a myth; and the notion of fixed and definite solutions is dismissed because it is said to ignore the dynamic and ambiguous character of all human things. As far as discourse analysis is concerned, collectivism is always oppressive because it won't tolerate diversity or aberration. Foucault writes as if from the French Revolution to the Gulag, the practical effect of collective political action waged in the name of emancipation and freedom has been terror. As so often with his writings, the argument depends upon the use of extreme examples. However, the general principle that the discourse of collectivism (whether of a Marxist, feminist, or nationalist type) creates witch hunts and punishes dissent is readily comprehended and is very familiar to social workers who use the labelling perspective in their work.

Discourse analysis encourages social workers to take a positive view of diversity. Attempts to centralise or standardise human behaviour are regarded with suspicion. Deviance, in particular, is interpreted not as meaningless or senseless, but rather as informative behaviour which exposes 'normality' as a specific construction of discipline and control. Moreover, discourse analysis encourages the social worker to regard relations of social work as relations of power, i.e. relations which are both enabling and constraining, liberating and repressive. This is advanced as a corrective to traditional social work which tends to overestimate the positive side of social work intervention and marginalise the regulatory aspects of practice. In addition it is intended to counter the radical tendency which sees progressive change in terms of total, positive transformation. It might be said that discourse analysis urges social workers to break out of the stifling complacency of traditionalism and the hubris of radicalism.

Discourse analysis has political effects, but it has scrupulously avoided formulating a political programme. Its linguistically grounded model of power suggests that the shape and effects of power can change. The emergence of 'the social' in the nineteenth century is a good example of a massive power shift in the system of discipline and control. The development of a new network of allowances and benefits to provide compensation for illness, old age, and unemployment, and new relays of caring and helping occupations associated with social work is said to have produced a more thorough, more penetrating system of regulation. However, power is seen finally as irreducible: there is no life without power, no social work without regulation. Thus, the social worker is required to oppose the *doxa* and all forces which propound the view that power is centred on a subject, that individuals are self-determining, that fixed meanings exist, that symptoms can be traced to their original causes, that problems can be definitely and conclusively solved, and that abnormality is absolute. As Foucault observes, discourse analysis struggles to avoid the conclusion that,

> this then is what needs to be done. It should be an instrument for those who fight, those who resist and refuse what is. Its use should be in processes of conflict and confrontation, essays in refusal. It doesn't have to lay down the law. It isn't a stage in programming. It is a challenge directed to what is.
>
> (Foucault 1981: 13)

Thus discourse analysis leads social work to the task of permanent deconstructive criticism. The social worker is called upon to be the indefatigable opponent of the various delusions of power. Familiar and specialised ideas of normality, consent, care, need, cure, etc., are probed to breaking point and beyond. Developmental models of social work are subjected to counterpoint and paradox. Legislative power is unpeeled, tested, and sometimes shredded. Above all, social work is social criticism.

5

'The social' in social work

Only in modern societies does one find a category of workers, trained and empowered, who expend paid labour in social caring and helping. Traditional societies rely on informal family and community networks to cope with serious emotional and practical problems in everyday life. Moreover, help and care are usually dispensed in the context of powerful religious beliefs which impose a strong responsibility upon the group to care for distressed individuals and sanction social intervention. In contrast, modern societies are marked by features of pluralism, secularism, complex occupational divisions, a money economy, and the concentration of populations in towns and cities. These features are reflected in the particular qualities of social transactions in modern societies. Social transactions tend to be impersonal, episodic, and changeful.

We will return to these features later in the chapter when we consider the relevance of modernism for social work. Here it is sufficient to note the general point that the circumstances of modern life mean that many people experience everyday life as *decentred* subjects. That is, they feel isolated and drifting with only loose affiliations to the family, community, and nation. Complaints of rootlessness and loneliness are very familiar to social workers. Abandoned wives, rejected lovers, members of social minorities, and the unemployed figure prominently in urban caseloads. Here the feelings of rootlessness and loneliness exist in concentrated form. In bringing the need for help into contact with the desire to help, society has created a sensitive borderline area of social life: *the social*. We mentioned it in the last chapter in the course of our discussion of 'the disciplinary society'. We shall devote the whole of the next section to describing it more fully.

What is 'the social'?

Donzelot defines the social as 'the set of means which allow social life to escape material pressures and politico-moral uncertainties; the entire range of methods which make the members of society relatively safe' (1979: xxvi). The social therefore includes the complete range of allowances and benefits to provide compensation for unemployment, illness, and old age; and the practices of assistance associated with social work and the other 'helping professions'.

We are not concerned here to trace the historical origins of the social. Although we are obliged to note in passing the obvious influence of Christianity and humanism in creating a social space in which the individual can escape from 'material processes and politico-material uncertainties'. Turner's work on personal disclosure and confession draws a direct link between the Christian confessional and the emergence of the social. In his words:

> The assumptions of the [Christian] confessional – the culture of guilt, the criteria of the true confession, the innocence of the talk, the interior conscience – are through a process of secularisation redistributed in a network of modern institutions. The confession did not decline or disappear; it was redeployed in psychoanalysis, police practice, court procedure, modern literature and medicine.
>
> (Turner 1984: 218-19)

We have little to add to these words save to say that the network of modern institutions obviously also encompasses social work (see also Hepworth and Turner 1982). Any description of the social must begin by observing that it involves the relaxation of the general prohibitions which govern social relations. 'Normal' everyday life represses deep emotions. Work and community life provide few opportunites for people to communicate their deepest fears and anxieties directly to strangers. The social recognises this. It encourages the exchange of repression for openness and tolerance. People are encouraged to talk frankly about themselves and their problems. Unmet needs are articulated, intimate fears and wants are faced.

In secular society, the social is an altar of self-disclosure. However, unlike acts of self-disclosure which occur in private with loved ones, the social is firmly part of the public domain. The client speaks in confidentiality, but he speaks to a representative of the state who is vested with legal powers. Communication in the social is organised to fulfil a therapeutic purpose. Through speech and other forms of self-disclosure (e.g. body language), inner problems are externalised. The social worker helps the client to make sense of problems which may appear at first sight to be senseless, and to find meaning in events which may appear to be meaningless. Following the practice of discourse analysis, it is helpful to think of communication in the social as a 'text' which is 'read' by the social worker. The assumption, of course, is that the social worker possesses theoretical insights into the nature of personal problems which the client either lacks or represses. Consider the following passage:

> Ask a withdrawn, distressed child what is the matter, and one is likely to get the reply, 'Nothing'. Translated, that means, 'Quite a lot, and it goes fairly deep, but I don't know whether I can trust you with it at the moment, so I'm not going to tell you, because I'm safer with my own hurt than sharing it with someone who might use it against me.'
>
> (Atherton 1986: 50)

What additional light does this passage throw on the nature of the social? Three points must be made. In the first place, a distinction is made between the immediate appearance of things and underlying reality. Communication in the social involves getting behind appearances and excavating reality which resides 'fairly deep' beneath the surface. The second point is that the social work task is associated with discovering authenticity. The social worker's 'reading' of the communication process is said to get to the truth of the matter. In contrast, the consciousness of the client is assumed, implicitly, and sometimes explicitly, to be confused or false. The third point is that the social is presented as a world of high trust relations. The client is urged to share intimate matters without fear of condemnation and rejection. The sincerity of relations in the social is contrasted with the low trust relations which characterise wider society, especially the world of work and cash transactions. For example, Rees (1978: 119) quotes the response of a teenage girl to her social worker: 'When I met her [the social worker] she was different. She treated me like a person whereas you're just a number at social security and they only deal with money.' The 'social' then, enables the individual to be treated as a 'real' person, someone with unique feelings, thoughts, experience, and requirements.

Moral panics and social work

Although the social possesses unique characteristics, it remains part of society. Indeed, as we sought to show in the last chapter, for the likes of Foucault and Donzelot it is an essential element of 'the disciplinary society'. The network of discourses on care and help which it supports is said to impose deeper, more effective systems of control over individual behaviour. The existence of the social recognises both the limits of family jurisdiction to deal with personal problems and the responsibility of the state to fill the breach. Precisely because the social is part of the public domain, it is subject to the scrutiny of society. If Foucault and Donzelot are right, the ultimate *raison d'être* of the social is to prevent the irruption of 'abnormal' or 'unhealthy' acts. It follows that the social reaction against social workers is most intense when such acts occur.

Cohen (1972) devised the concept of 'moral panic' to signify a focused social reaction to behaviour which is labelled as disruptive or potentially disruptive of 'order', 'normality', and 'social health'. Moral panics are adversarial. They attribute culpability to the agent accused of disrupting normality, and/or incompetence to the agent or agents charged with the task of preventing disruption. Furthermore, moral panics are basically conservative reactions. Their basic aim is to restore order, normality, and health rather than to examine critically the validity of these social categories in 'our' social life. Waves of moral panic have swept over social work in recent years. Social workers have been accused, among other things, of bumbling inefficiency, gullibility, spinelessness, and lethargy. As the BASW *Annual Review 1985-86* observed, somewhat euphemistically: 'Social work still has problems with its public image and many are still unaware of what we do and why' (BASW 1986: 3).

Moral panics in social work have occurred in respect of care of the elderly, the mentally handicapped, drug addicts, alcoholics, and the unemployed. However, nowhere have the panics been more severe, nowhere more unremitting, than in cases of child abuse. For example, late in 1985 the Blom-Cooper Report on the death of 2-year-old Jasmine Beckford (victim of her stepfather) was published. It identified serious errors on the part of social workers in handling the case. The report prompted a series of scathing attacks on social work in the press. The *Mail on Sunday* (8 December 1985) wrote luridly of 'bureaucrats shuffling and trailing their feet, while scapegoats get their throats cut, while the greasy ball of blame is passed swiftly from hand to hand.' Three Brent social workers were dismissed as a result of the Beckford case. This led to an unofficial strike by the local branch of NALGO which argued that the three social workers were being used as scapegoats and demanded their reinstatement. The action was partially successful as one of the three was eventually reinstated. However, the *Sunday Express* (8 December 1985) in a lead editorial on the strike commented,

> they care much about their job security, those NALGO members who have gone on unofficial strike in Brent. They care about their pay and their pensions and their status. But there is one person they plainly care not one toss about. And that one person is Jasmine Beckford. ... Theirs is an action which spits on the idea of individual responsibility, on duty to the public and on justice for a little girl who is dead.

More recently the murder of 4-year-old Kimberley Carlile (by her stepfather) provoked a full-scale moral panic against social work. Social workers were accused of 'abandoning' Kimberley (*Today*, 16 May 1987). *The Sunday Times* (17 May 1987) dismissed social workers as being too easily 'fobbed off'. The *Daily Mirror* (16 May 1987) alleged that social workers were guilty of 'mistake after mistake'. Interestingly, the *Daily Mail* focused explicitly on the language of social work in its condemnation. Referring to the court testimony of the senior social worker involved in the case, it reported:

> There he was in court, speaking about interaction when he meant talking, cohabiting when he meant living in the same house and Kim's presentation when he meant her behaviour. How can anybody have any confidence in a training that forces people to speak such phoney, meaningless tripe?
> (*Daily Mail*, 20 May 1987)

The language of social work is presented as intrinsically remote from the real world, a source of confusion, hesitation, and mystification. Moreover, this unsatisfactory state of affairs is contrasted with a picture of child care in the years before the Seebohm Report (1968) and the era of the generic social worker:

> Then the old-fashioned NSPCC officer was usually a burly ex-serviceman speaking a plain language, afraid of nobody, frequently working on instinct, a gut feeling that things weren't right, and with his mind unclogged with the jargon and claptrap social workers get bogged down by.
>
> (*Daily Mail*, 20 May 1987)

The ease and fluency with which moral panics against social work swing into action in the media suggest the existence of a deep reservoir of negative energy in the public mind against social work. We shall come to the reasons for this presently. At this point in our discussion we wish to note that the negative energy in the public mind has been regularly topped up with a trickle of dismissive academic studies on social work. In the 1980s, with the advent of the New Right the trickle has turned into a torrent. Criticism has taken two main forms. In the first place, social workers are attacked for their alleged *technical* insufficiencies. For example, Brewer and Lait (1980) submit that social workers are lax in monitoring progress and vague in formulating the precise objectives of practice. Similarly, Flew (1985: 236) charges social workers with spouting 'gouts of ... lordly and etherial guff' on the nature of the social work task, at the cost of the real business of practical care. The second main form which criticism of social work has assumed refers to the *culture* of caring and helping. A variety of studies have attacked the welfare mentality of state planning in the post-war years. The provision of social security is held to have diverted scarce resources from wealth-creating investment (Harris and Seldon 1979; Friedman and Friedman 1980). Furthermore, it is alleged to have produced an unhealthy addiction to state hand-outs among the people. This is said to be expressed tangibly in the general decline of the spirit of enterprise and the spread of lethargic, work-shy attitudes among the workforce. Implicitly, welfarism is associated with infantilism. In the work of Carroll the link is made explicit:

> It is expected today that the State will dress any wound and soothe any slight. If we become unemployed it will pay

us; if our company goes bankrupt it will prop us up; if we become ill it will care for us; if we don't want to look after aged or handicapped kin it will provide institutions for them; if flood or fire strike our town it will rebuild it for us; if our wives desert us it will send a social worker to hold our hands. In all of this it behaves like the loving and non-judging mother, as it is expected to do. The corollary is that it encourages us to remain children, dependent and without responsibility for what we do.

(Carroll 1985: 174)

The allegation that the social perpetuates attitudes of dependency and lack of responsibility is by no means confined to right-wing commentators. The neo-Marxist historian and pundit of culture Christopher Lasch (1980: 224-32) identifies the growth of the welfare state with the rise of 'the new paternalism'. Drawing heavily on the thought of Donzelot, Lasch argues that legislation in the late nineteenth and twentieth centuries has weakened the power of the family to produce self-reliant 'rugged individuals'. Instead power has been ceded to the health and welfare professionals who are said to have provided cosseting rather than progressive help for those judged to be 'in need of care'. Again, one cannot go far into the literature without observing the powerful role that received ideas and moralistic language play in the business of establishing and defending positions. Writing of the New Right attack on welfarism, Bean *et al.* are drawn magnetically to comment on the 'uncritically simplistic formulae encapsulated in slogans of the likes of "privatisation" or "free market" or "self help and enterprise", almost as if the mouthing of such phrases could magically produce the solution to complex welfare problems' (1985: xii). It is most important to add that the weakness is not limited to the New Right. It also leaps out in the slogans of left-wingers who argue that real welfare care is merely a matter of 'collectivism', or the 'end of class society'.

Death and 'the social'

The depiction of the social as an environment of cosy, relaxed, and secure intimacy is misleading. The attempt to relax prohibitions in the client always carries the risk of misfiring. In most cases, entering the social brings the client release from troubling emotional tensions. However, it can also create a situation in which the social worker becomes the focus of client aggression. Between 1984 and 1986 three social workers in Britain were murdered in the course of their duties. In order to illustrate the aggression which is latent in the social let us refer briefly to these cases.

On 5 September 1986, in the Quinton district of Birmingham, Brian Wildman strangled his estranged wife Julie and held her body under bath water. He then waited for Miss Frances Betteridge, a senior children's welfare officer, to arrive for a home visit. When she did, Wildman attacked her with a Stanley knife. Miss Betteridge succeeded in disarming him but was knocked unconscious in the process. Wildman strangled Miss Betteridge and took her body to the bathroom where he immersed it under water for some minutes. He then dragged both bodies to the main bedroom, put on a jacket and went to the local school to collect his twin 5-year-old sons. He returned to the house, laid the twins down on a bed and, after starting a number of fires in the house, lay down with them. When the boys started screaming, he smashed a window and they were rescued by neighbours. Wildman pleaded guilty to murdering the women and was arrested outside the house. He is reported to have told the police:

I was angry, uptight. I thought she [Betteridge] had been doing things behind my back with Julie about the kids. She was saying, 'The boys love you. We're not going to take the boys off you.' But I didn't believe her.

(*Guardian*, 18 December 1986)

In the summer of 1984 Isabel Schwarz was employed as a residential social worker at Bexley hospital in Kent. The bulk of her work consisted of clients suffering from mental illness. In the early evening of 8 July she was working alone in the social services office, a room isolated from the main medical complex. Miss Schwarz was last seen by her secretary who left for home at 5 p.m. When she failed to arrive for a meeting with a colleague later in the evening, he drove to the office to find out what had happened. When he arrived he found Miss Schwarz's body. She had been stabbed repeatedly. Two days later a female, former hospital inmate, who had been a client of the dead social worker, was arrested and charged with the murder. The accused was brought to trial but was found unfit to plead. Since that time she has been confined to Broadmoor mental hospital.

The third murder occurred in April 1985. Norma Morris, a Haringey social worker, called to assess a man for admission to mental hospital. The assessment never took place. She was found in the house at the foot of the stairs in a pool of blood. She had suffered multiple skull fractures, she had been stabbed repeatedly, and an attempt had been made to sever her head. The Haringey assistant social services director of the time was later quoted as saying: 'There was no way anyone could have prevented the violence. This is a risk business and we cannot remove all risk. People have to accept that and be conscious of it' (*Guardian*, 10 November 1986).

It is not possible to give accurate figures on incidents of violence against social workers. Statistics depend upon self-reporting, and many social workers decide not to report physical attacks. However, it is a safe bet that violence against social workers is much higher than in comparable helping professions such as teaching, medicine, and the law. Why is this? It is necessary to make three points.

First, and most obviously, much social work is conducted in isolation from other co-workers. A teacher who is threatened with attack in the classroom may call for assistance. But a social worker on a home visit or residential assignment usually spends long periods of time alone with the client. Most social service departments have no formal policy on reducing the risk of attack. However, since the three murders described here, there is growing pressure from social workers for social service departments to arrange more joint visiting of clients and to provide staff with effective means of communication such as personal alarms and/or cordless telephones.

Second, most fieldworkers in social work are women. It is short-sighted to see violence in social work merely in terms of isolated attacks made by disturbed clients against professional workers. The overwhelming majority of client attacks in social work involve male violence against women. The male client reacts not merely to being advised what to do, or confronted with the emotional, social, and legal consequences of a given state of affairs; he reacts to being advised and confronted by a woman. It is not superfluous to note here that the three social workers murdered in Britain between 1984 and 1986 were all women.

Third, it is necessary to state plainly that social work is dangerous work. The social worker regularly comes into contact with clients who are emotionally distraught and angry. The received view in traditional social work is that professional work skills, such as building empathy and a climate of confidence in the social work relationship, should be sufficient to avoid serious life-threatening situations. Because of this ideological position, training in self-defence has never been a significant part of qualifying courses in the UK. However, there is now reason to suppose that the received view is over-optimistic. Social workers, especially in deprived inner-city areas, do face personal risks. Moreover, there is growing pressure from basic grade workers for social service departments to run in-service courses in self-defence.

The quest for community

Historically speaking, the development of the social in social work is a product of a spirit of liberation. It arose as an attempt to break free of the taboos and thoughtless moral and social prejudices of modern industrial life. Moreover, it aimed to create an environment of close, authentic relationships between social workers and clients. The social was born because informal family and community systems of care and help were thought to be deficient. The family was often too involved emotionally with the person in distress to see the wood for the trees. As for the community, it was thought to lack the objective knowledge which full-time welfare workers could bring to the management of social and personal problems.

The attempt to overcome the barriers of intimacy created an environment of organised intimacy which we have called the social. Yet, as the professionalisation and scale of social work has grown, the value of the social has been increasingly contested. In a reversal of the original pioneering argument, the family and community are now widely venerated as havens of closeness, openness, and intimacy.[1] In contrast, the social is presented as an artificial, alienating side of life in which inflexibility, officiousness, and cant exist cheek by jowl. It is somewhere in which good intentions have gone terribly wrong. The antidote and cure is to unfetter the good intentions of ordinary people – to enable people to help and care for each other 'naturally' in the 'elemental' units of society: the family and the community.

The idea of community care is not new. In Britain, Finch and Groves (1980) trace the legislative origins back to the National Health Service Act (1946) and the National Assistance Act (1948).

Both Acts made provision for developing community care in the personal social services. Furthermore, the idea was perpetuated in the years up to the 1980s through legislation and policy on care for the mentally ill and elderly. However, it really came into its own in the 1980s, with the attack on the liberal consensus on the welfare state. Community care is seen as a more 'natural', 'real' form of care, helping those in adversity and responding more sensitively to their unique needs than the state welfare services. Moreover, policy-makers favour it as a low-cost option in welfare management: it extends the commitment to care in society without placing additional demands on the public purse. Feminist writers have criticised the idea of community care on the grounds that it operates with the tacit, and sometimes explicit, assumption that women will take up the additional burden of caring work (see Wilson 1977; Finch and Groves 1980). This is a shrewd and valid argument. The concept of community care is indeed representative of the sexism which underlies much thinking about welfare in modern society. Yet it also touches on wider cultural and historical issues.

In our view the concept of community care is, above all, a romantic one. It is defined in opposition to the large-scale, impersonal, episodic conditions of modern urban-industrial life. It harks back to the village ideal. That is, it imagines community life in the present to be a duplicate of the principles of belonging and sharing that are said to characterise preindustrial social life. In the village ideal, everyone knows each other and neighbours band together to assist someone who is in distress. The reasons for this social cohesion are not hard to understand. Low levels of social and geographical mobility, and the primitive interdependence of people for their security, consumption, and amusement, combined to create the conditions for high levels of solidarity. These conditions no longer exist. Most people today are mobile. Few of us live in the house of our birth. Few of us follow the same paid work as our parents. We live in towns and cities, often as strangers to the people who live in the same apartment block or street.

Yet, undeniably, the idea of community still has a strong pull. Sennett (1977) has written with distinction on the quest for community in modern times. He argues that city planners and welfare managers make extravagant claims on behalf of community life in urban settings. The village ideal has been destroyed by the generalised geographical and social mobility found in modern society and by the spread of individualism, pluralism, and privacy.

Moreover, he concludes that the quest for community today delivers exactly the opposite of what it promises:

> Modern community seems to be about fraternity in a dead, hostile world; it is in fact all too often an experience of fratricide. ... Who 'we' are becomes a highly selective act of imagination: one's immediate neighbours, co-workers in the office, one's family. Identifying with people one doesn't know, people who are strangers but who share one's ethnic interests, family problems or religion becomes hard.
>
> (Sennett 1977: 304-10)

In Chapter 4 we noted that for Foucault, the main paradox of humanist welfare management is that determining the needs and rights of citizens necessarily restricts the freedom of the individual (see pp.133-6). By extension, Foucault implies that the regulation of welfare and need will engender resistance as well as assent. The passage from Sennett's book suggests that forms of community planning and community care do not overcome the paradox: they compound it. For the community is possessive and territorial. Belonging to it carries with it the obligation of recognising differences with other communities. Making a place for oneself and one's 'own' community necessarily deprives other people and other communities of that space and the rights and obligations that go with it. Nowhere is this clearer than in the official institutions of community life. It is a great mistake to see Community Action Groups and Neighbourhood Watch Schemes as evidence of the vitality of communal life. They are predicated in motives of self-interest rather than solidarity. They arise out of the desire to protect one's own property and immediate environment from the intrusions of the city hall, private capital, and the criminal underclass rather than out of deep-rooted collective sentiment.

Sennett places the concept of community firmly in society, that is in the totality of cultural and material relations that exist between people. For him, there can be no idea of community without the corresponding idea of interests. The idea of interests leads logically to the idea of power and, with this, to the whole framework of class, patriarchy, ethnicity, bureaucracy, etc., which shapes social action and, of course, is shaped by it.

It is instructive to compare Sennett's approach with the stock ideas of professional social work. Consider a document like the influential Barclay Report (1982). Throughout its pages there is a heavy emphasis on community-orientated social work. Yet the meaning of community is strangely disembodied and abstract. This may be illustrated by the vocabulary used in the report. Communities are defined as 'networks of informal, reciprocal relationships' (1982: 199). Their foundation and existence are discussed in purely formal terms. Thus, communities are said to be forged by blood (kinship), property (geographical proximity), production (occupation), or the receiving of goods and services (consumption). Several points arise from this description. Here we will concentrate upon three of them.

To begin with, it is surely short-sighted to imply that communities exist wherever the formal attributes of community life are established. To put it differently, the mere fact of physical location (a neighbourhood, a work-place, a recreation area) is no guarantee that the values of communal life (closeness, neighbourliness, intimacy) will prevail. For example, a regular complaint made by people living in the new housing estates and satellite towns built in the urban development programmes of the post-war years is that they are trapped in lonely, soulless settlements which lack any focus for real solidarity.

A second point is that the Barclay Report treats communities as if they are so many pieces of a jigsaw which together make up 'Society'. This view of communities and society is excessively harmonistic and bland. It ignores those forms of social life which are antagonistic to the host community and reject the values of the surrounding society. Thus, Hebdige (1979), commenting on modern subcultural forms in Britain, identifies groups which are hostile to mainstream British culture 'from within'. One such group is West Indian youth who reject the materialism, conservatism, and racism of British society and ritualise a lifestyle built on 'roots' in an 'imagined elsewhere' (Africa, the West Indies). Other groups take the traditional values of the host community and surrounding society and use them as materials to challenge or subvert the status quo. Hebdige asks us to consider the case of punks. They took the insignia of traditional Britishness (the Queen, the Union Jack, etc.) and juxtaposed them with 'nameless housing estates, anonymous dole queues, slums-in-the-abstract' (Hebdige 1979: 65).

Mention of the challenge to the meaning of community raises the question of the language of enthusiasm and hope which surrounds the idea of community. This brings us to our third and final point. In the Barclay Report and elsewhere in traditional social work the term 'community' conjures up powerful and evocative images of warmth, belonging, and sharing. These are gilded images in our culture. They are associated with our 'nature', 'the good society', our 'peace of mind'. So much is this the case that to feel their absence from our lives is to feel onerously deprived, a victim. Yet paradoxically, many of our common everyday acts of sharing and belonging inspire feelings of resentment in us. We object to the taxation of our income not only because it takes our money away, but also because it allows others either to spend or to receive what is not theirs. We like to feel that we belong to our neighbours but feel put upon if we are faced with too many demands for helping, caring, and participating. The language that we use to express our sense of place and responsibilities to others seems clumsy:

> Words like fraternity, belonging and community are so soaked in nostalgia and utopianism that they are nearly useless as guides to the real possibilities of solidarity in modern society. *Modern life has changed the possibilities of civic solidarity and our language stumbles behind like an overburdened porter with a mountain of old cases.*
>
> (Ignatieff 1984: 138; our emphasis)

Crisis points

Ignatieff's words, like Sennett's before him, refer to a cultural crisis: the generalised condition in a society in which words no longer match meanings. Like the discourse theorists that we examined in Chapter 4, he argues that our official language of care ascribes feelings to us that we don't feel. Logically consistent with this proposition is the idea that the received language of care performs an important, conservative illusion in society. It consoles us with the belief that something is being done to relieve distress and oppression. Yet the language long ago ceased to be an effective lever for change. Instead it has become a mere end in itself. Edelman (1977) and Cohen (1985) make the point when they refer to the 'professional babble' and 'control-talk' of the helping professions. Such arguments equate the official language of social work with a placebo which gives the comfort of real thought and real action about what is wrong but is, in fact, a substitute for both. In Chapters 2 and 3 we looked at examples from Marxist and feminist positions in social work which make this case. The reader may refer back to these pages for further details (see expecially pp.53-69;100-10).

Crisis is, of course, a well-worn phrase in social work. Social workers frequently refer to 'crisis cases'. Furthermore, 'crisis intervention' has developed as a distinctive, specialised approach to cope with crisis problems. However, it would be wrong to infer that the term is simply used to describe the condition of some clients. As we have noted again and again in this book, the profession of social work is in crisis. Society harbours profound doubts about the value of social work, and social workers themselves are at odds about their role and purpose in modern society.

The sense of crisis is real and pervasive. However, the terms which social workers use to discuss crisis are almost always parochial. They exemplify a tendency to think atomistically about social problems and to analyse crises as isolated episodes. That particular crises derive their character as parts of larger wholes is a view that is alien to traditional ways of thinking in social work. When the idea does take hold, as is the case with Marxist and feminist writers, analysis too often slides into reification: all action is 'explained' as a reflection of giant overarching systems such as the class structure or patriarchy.

Matters of class and patriarchy are obviously central to social work. But so are matters of culture and language, and they have been given a much lower profile in the social work literature. In our criticisms of Marxist and feminist social work, and in our discussion of discourse analysis, we sought to redress this wrong. Rather than talk of one system and one crisis in social work, we prefer to talk of many systems and many crises. Moreover, rather than analyse what happens to clients in terms of their relation to a single system of power, we prefer to analyse what happens in terms of the interaction between systems of power. Of course, we realise that to say this much commits us to a wider view of why social problems develop and how the world works. We devote the whole of the next section to elaborating this view and spelling out its relevance for social work.

Modernism and social work

To begin with, a frank observation: merely to raise the matter of modernism and social work is to crave the reader's indulgence.

160

In recent years, social workers have been invited to locate their activities in the context of (a) capitalist society, (b) patriarchal society, and (c) the community. Such grand claims have been made on behalf of each concept, often by writers who are not full-time social workers and sometimes by writers who have never set foot in an agency office, that to press for the concept of modernism here might seem like adding insult to injury. Still, if we are to see social work as something more than a series of unrelated episodes, it is necessary to postulate a context which gives activity shape. It is our dissatisfaction with attempts to situate social work in the context of capitalist society, patriarchy, and community that led us to search for a more valid context. That search led to modernism.

Modernism is often confused with modernisation. There are indeed close parallels between the two. Nevertheless, a fairly clear set of distinctions can be made. Modernisation refers to the process by which societies acquire modern structural features such as industrial economies, urban populations, bureaucratic systems of organisation, national audio-visual communications networks, and complex occupational divisions. Modernism refers to the type of social consciousness which is characteristic of modern societies: a form of social consciousness which views itself and the world as dynamic, many-sided, fragmentary, and discontinuous. Modernisation increases the velocity of life; it challenges traditional order and religion; through science it shatters and dissolves all firmly held belief; through the money economy and the commercialisation of products and experience it reduces all value to cash value. These processes, which transform social conditions, are consistent with modernism.

Although modernism is an abstraction, its influence can be studied quite concretely. When clients come to social workers because their lives have been wrecked through sudden and unexpected divorce or unemployment, when they feel immobilised by loneliness or the impersonality of the conditions around them, when they feel that nothing makes sense and that nothing will ever make sense again, they exemplify key aspects of modernist sensibility. Similarly, when social workers discount textbook precedent or the protocol of the office in dealing with referrals, when they are unable to choose between several courses of action because each one seems to be equally right, equally helpful, for the clients' well-being, when they feel that referrals come from nowhere, in an endless stream, with problems that have no solution, they can be studied as illustrations of modernism.

From these few words it is apparent that the experience of modernism is often one of ambiguity and frustration. This is expressed metaphorically in language. We say that our language traps us, ties us in knots, or turns what we mean upside-down. Throughout the book we have given examples of received ideas in social work which are presented as clear and definitive in theory and training, but turn out to be opaque and ambivalent in practice. We are thinking, in particular, of ideas like acceptance, trust, respect, resistance, and defence mechanism in traditional social work; and ideas like collectivism, consciousness-raising, alienation, commitment, and liberation in radical social work. The fact that modernism gives a high profile to the ambiguity and dynamism of communication suggests that 'effective intervention' and 'problem-solving exercise' are hazardous claims for social workers to make. However, modernism does not dismiss problem-solving *tout court*. Rather it suggests that all solutions are relative, interim, and subject to radical change. There can be no fixed and definite solution to a problem because there is no fixed and definite order in society.

Although modernism signifies a categoric form of social consciousness it must also be evaluated within a historical view of human consciousness. Now, it is foolish to try to establish points of origin or thresholds when discussing deep changes in social consciousness. All that can be said with certainty about the rise of modernism is that between the closing decades of the nineteenth century and the end of the First World War modernism arose to the fore. In these years technological innovations such as the telephone, wireless telegraph, X-ray, cinema, bicycle, automobile, and airplane come through; moreover, cultural developments including psychoanalysis, cubism, steel and glass skyscrapers, the free-form novel, and the theory of relativity all occurred at this time. They contributed to the transformation in the conditions of life, and the effects continue to resonate in our relations today.

To talk of 'deep change' and 'transformation' necessarily raises the question of what preceded modernism. Here we are faced with an immediate difficulty. To examine the dominant form of social consciousness in the pre-modernist period would require a full-length study. Such an exercise falls well beyond the scope of this book. We can do no more than provide a limited illustration of this form and note its expression in welfare and social work. With the limited nature of our discussion understood, let us make the following general points.

While there are many counter-arguments, notably the divisions within classes between 'progressive' and 'conservative' values and the increasing challenge posed by working-class movements, it is widely agreed that the years from 1770 to 1910 are the years of bourgeois society (Lowe 1982; Kern 1983; Corrigan and Sayer 1985). How, in a few words, can we characterise bourgeois society? To begin with, it was a male-dominated society which required the economic and erotic subordination of women. In addition, it was economically reliant upon the exploitation of the working class and colonial labour. The principal economic and moral value of this society was individualism. 'Men' were held to be free to pursue their interests providing they advanced the good of society. In Bentham's utilitarianism we have the main philosophical expression of this position. Man is presented as a dualistic being: a creature who seeks to gain pleasure and avoid pain. Bentham maintained that all human action can be assessed according to the degree to which it either increased or decreased the sum of human happiness. The task of the philosopher, continued Bentham, is to formulate the moral principles governing society into a set of practical rules which can enable people to decide infallibly the worth of every human action.

Note the enormous, untested assumptions underpinning this position. It is assumed that 'man' consists of common undifferentiated properties: the desire to acquire pleasure and avoid pain. It is assumed that experiences of pleasure and pain can be determined objectively, much as the price of a commodity is determined objectively in the economic market. It is assumed that the interests of the individual and the interests of society coincide. It is assumed that class, gender, race, etc., play little part in how a person ultimately sees the world and what is judged to be pleasurable and painful, 'virtuous' or 'harmful'. Consider carefully the psychological characteristics associated with this position. It is assumed that decisions are made through the rational calculation of costs and benefits. It is assumed that nature and society exist as resources for human domination. It is assumed that it is normal and natural for the individual to compete with others in order to gain personal profit.

Bourgeois society was a class society. Marx characterised it as a society based on the domination of the working class by the bourgeois class. Lowe (1982) maintains that the hierarchy of class domination carried over into the general perception of the world.

163

Thus, people saw the world as hierarchically ordered and events in the world as parts of a linear chain of cause and effect. Of course, the absolutist court societies of the eighteenth century and before were also hierarchically ordered. However, their view of hierarchy distinguished many more levels of power than the bourgeois world view. There were good material reasons for this view. Court society indeed consisted of a complicated network of estates in which numerous titular distinctions signified vast gradations of power. In bourgeois society these gradations remain, but they are overtaken and dominated by a series of fundamental dualisms, e.g. bosses/workers, rich/poor, industrious/idle, civilised society/the mob. It is through these divisions that people in bourgeois society struggle to make sense of the world.

Talk of 'the hierarchically ordered world' and 'the perception of the linear chain of cause and effect' may try the patience of the reader who wants to know what all of this has to do with the crisis in social work and the concrete problems that he or she faces in the area team or residential work setting. We sympathise with this point of view and we will try to make the links explicit in what follows. However, the radical nature of our argument requires us to pave our way carefully. We are arguing that social work theory and practice, in both its traditional and radical (Marxist/feminist) forms, cannot get to grips with the emotional and social problems that modernism perpetuates. It is in this spirit of building our argument carefully that we offer the following two examples of the bourgeois world view. The examples refer, first, to the bourgeois view of welfare and, second, to the bourgeois view of poverty.

In bourgeois society personal welfare was said to be a matter for the conduct of the individual rather than the conduct of society. A distinction was made between 'the deserving poor' and 'the work-shy'. The deserving poor were to be raised above their condition and through the principles of self-help placed on the path of self-reliance. As for the so-called work-shy, things were left to take their natural course. As Carlyle put it:

> For the idle man there is no place in this England of ours. He that will not work, and save according to his means, let him go elsewither; let him know that for *him* the law has made no soft provision, but a hard and stern one. ... He that will not work according to his faculty, let him perish according to his necessity: there is no juster law than that.
>
> (Cited in Himmelfarb 1984: 194)

What strikes one today is the fierce two-dimensionality of these words. Welfare claimants are required to adopt 'voluntarily' the cardinal bourgeois moral and economic values, or submit to something close to genocide. A dualistic welfare policy, indeed!

Bourgeois society demanded that the working class make themselves in the image of the bourgeoisie. This, of course, involved raising working-class living standards and extending property ownership. However, bourgeois society stopped well short of advocating the elimination of poverty. On the contrary, for the individual who wished to get on, poverty could be an asset. For example, Smiles, writing in 1859, speculated that,

> so far from poverty being a misfortune, it may, by vigorous self-help, be converted even into a blessing; rousing a man to that struggle with the world in which, though some may purchase ease by degradation, the right-minded and true-hearted find strength, confidence and triumph.
>
> (Smiles 1986: 33)

This brings us to our second point. Bourgeois society attributed a functional role to poverty. For Smiles, as we have seen, it was a spur to self-help. For Andrew Carnegie, the self-made millionaire and noted philanthropist, it was the basis for the advancement of civilisation: 'To abolish honest, industrious self denying poverty would be to destroy the soil upon which mankind produces the virtues which enable our race to reach still higher civilisation than it now possesses' (Carnegie 1896: 83-4). Note the ease with which the language of bourgeois society reifies its subject and dignifies its object. Carnegie's words turn the poor into mere engine grease to oil the capitalist growth machine, and justify the conversion as a contribution to higher civilisation!

We have gone through some major points quite briefly. So let us summarise and highlight our argument. We live under modernism. Modernist consciousness is sensitive to the restlessness of life, the ambiguity of meaning, the relativity and diversity of things, the contingencies of action, and the lack of social consensus. Moreover, in modern society, work is not necessarily the central life interest, social roles are not binding and inflexible, and care is not necessarily tied to need. Modernism was preceded by a very different type of social consciousness: the consciousness of bourgeois society. In bourgeois society the world is presented as orderly and rule-bound; meaning is said to be fixed and definite;

human beings are thought to be composed of common needs and desires; play is subordinate to work; sexuality is officially confined to relationships of adult, heterosexual, married, lifelong, procreative union; each thing in society is given a place and a function, for example, there can be no rich without the poor, no worker without the employer, no law-abiding class without a criminal class, no sane without the insane.

Earlier, we dated bourgeois society as spanning the years between 1770 and 1910. After reading our account of bourgeois social consciousness, some readers may take exception to this distancing in time. Scan current state welfare policies in Britain, the USA, and the other western economies, and you will find copious reference to 'social security hand-outs' which 'price people out of work', the need for 'less dependence' on state welfare services, the desirability of 'more enterprising and resourceful' attitudes among the poor. In short, the air seems thick with support for Victorian values.

Such an impression appears to give scant comfort to a thesis which purports to show the end of bourgeois society. Yet we neither reject the impression nor disclaim the thesis. To say that bourgeois society has come to an end, as we do, is very different from saying that the bourgeois class has disappeared. It is a great but common mistake to equate the end of historical period with the cessation of all its institutions and influences. After all, the age of monarchy is dead, but we still have kings and queens; the law recognises equal rights for women, but women workers are concentrated in the low-paid, menial, part-time job sector; racial inequality is officially banned but prejudice against black people remains palpable and widespread. We could go on with more examples, but these are perhaps enough to establish the general point.

Modernism and bourgeois society

The bourgeois class remains a force in society. How could it be otherwise? For they managed the modernisation process and created the world in their own image. Yet their power is a pale version of its former self. The sense of natural justice and innate order has gone. Modernism has undermined bourgeois society. Consider Smiles's doctrine of self-help. Smiles built his doctrine on three principles: (a) the sanctity of family life; (b) the dignity of industry; (c) the necessity of personal solvency. Consider further the place of each principle in modern life.

Take the sanctity of family life. Undoubtedly, the virtues of the family are still extolled, and every adult is expected to find a partner, marry, and start a family. Yet compare this with our statistical knowledge of what is actually happening to marriage and family life in modern Britain. The number marrying for the first time fell by 6,000 to 257,000 between 1981 and 1985, while the percentage of women who were cohabiting rose from 5.6 to over 7 per cent. Illegitimate births rose from 81,000 to 126,000 and the percentage registered by both parents, suggesting a stable if unsanctified union, increased to 6.5 per cent of all births. By 1985, 5 per cent of people in the UK were living in one-parent families with dependent children. There were 150,000 abortions to British women in 1985, one for every five live births and 13,000 more than in 1980 (*Social Trends* 17 (1987)). The average duration of marriage in 1980 was 10.1 years; for couples with children it was 11.2 years and for those without children it was 7.8 years (*Social Trends* 13 (1983)). The 1981 census showed that 22 per cent of all households in the UK consisted of one person, 32 per cent of all households consisted of two people, and only 26 per cent of households corresponded to the nuclear family ideal of a married couple with one or two dependent children. Such figures suggest that statements affirming the sanctity of marriage and family life conflict with the reality of marriage and the family in modern Britain. Of course, the same might be said of statements in Victorian times. Our knowledge of this matter is incomplete because many abandoned wives in those years never reported their plight to an official authority. Nevertheless, we can say with certainty of modern times that many adults openly flaunt the received idea of 'normal', lifelong, married, procreative union in the conduct of their own lives.

The second principle underpinning Smiles's doctrine is the dignity of industry. He wrote: 'There is no discredit, but honour, in every walk of industry, whether it be tilling the ground, making tools, weaving fabrics, or selling the products behind the counter' (Smiles 1986: 189). Such words define work as the central life interest of individuals. We prove our worth to our neighbours and ourselves by what we make, what we sell, and what we earn. Yet in modern society, the enthusiasm for work is more instrumental, and the assumption that there is an innate dignity in industry is less secure. In the words of Gorz:

The traditional working class is now no more than a privileged minority. The majority of the population now belong to the post-industrial neo-proletariat which, with no job security or definite class identity, fills the area of probationary, contracted, casual, temporary and part-time employment ... [For them] work no longer signifies an activity or even a major occupation; it is merely a blank interval on the margins of life, to be endured in order to earn a little money.

(Gorz 1982: 69-70)

Gorz paints a bleak picture of a work-force under modernism which is progressively deskilled and replaced by automated machine processes. Pushing buttons, filling in forms, copying papers, sorting goods, number crunching – this is not intrinsically interesting work. For Gorz, the fact that the modern industrial worker sees work as a means to an end reflects a realistic assessment of the range of energies and faculties required in the modern work-place.

The third principle of Smiles's doctrine is the necessity of personal solvency. The individual is encouraged to seize opportunities and prosper, but only by cultivating a stringent economical attitude to time and money: 'Economy, at bottom, is but the spirit of order applied in the administration of domestic affairs: it means management, regularity, prudence, and the avoidance of waste. ... Every man ought so to contrive as to live within his means' (Smiles 1986: 184). The injunction to live within one's means remains a part of modern life. Yet it is monotonously and widely ignored. The modern appetite for credit and living beyond one's means is voracious. We don't so much avoid debt, as place our immediate debts under the stewardship of Access, American Express, Barclaycard, or our attentive bank manager. Like so much else in modern life, the received idea of generalised personal solvency turns out to be an illusion.

The shell of bourgeois society still surrounds us. For example, it is evident in the organisation of our forces of law and order, the educational curriculum that we offer our children, the administration of our social security system, and in much else besides. But it is a broken shell which exerts a fragile hold on our remaining consent. The old clichés, such as 'spend no more than you earn', 'waste not, want not', 'look after the pennies and the pounds will look after themselves', have a hollow ring in economies dominated by monopoly organisation, rampant consumerism, and adventure capital. Moreover, the existence of 'the social' is itself an affront to the old bourgeois sacred cow that family life is private and autonomous. It signifies the recognition of the public interest which overrides private rights. As Ellen Richards, a founder of modern social work in the USA, observed in arguing for the growth of professional social work: 'The child as a future citizen is an asset of the state, not the property of its parents. Hence its welfare is a direct concern of the state' (cited in Lasch 1980: 155).

The rise of 'the social' is both an agency and a symptom of modernism. It is an agency because the dispersal of power between representatives of the judiciary and social welfare outlets signifies the waning of power in the bourgeois family. The conduct of family life was always subject to the gaze of neighbours. However, with the rise of the social, it became subject to the gaze of society. Moreover, society armed the courts and social workers with legal powers to intervene in private family life and remove individuals judged to be 'at risk'.

'The social' is a symptom of modernism because it is an arena for substantial conflict, rapid change, and self-criticism. Conflict may be divided into the disagreements *between* social workers and other representatives of the social such as doctors, psychiatrists, magistrates, and the police, and the disagreements *among* social workers who represent conflicting traditions of theory and practice, e.g. casework, systems theory, Marxism, feminism. Critics of the social have often argued that it is a calculated strategy by the state to engineer compliance and propel 'the troubled client' back into normality. There is truth in this. However, it is a mistake to attribute a one-dimensional, conservative function to the social and leave it at that. The creation of an area in modern life dedicated to 'objective', 'professional' discourse on the nature of personal problems inevitably leads to conjecture on the conditions of society which nurture personal problems. Conjecture leads directly to criticism of the dominant economic, social, and moral order.

Under the influence of received ideas

An examination of critical consciousness in modern social work has occupied us for the greater part of the book. We have examined the major divisions within traditional social work and discussed the leading reactions of radical social work. Many of these reactions have emphasised that the roots of traditional social work lie deep in bourgeois society and, moreover, have played up the repressive and self-estranging effects of traditional practice. Yet we deceive ourselves if we imagine that radical social work has blasted out of the orbit of bourgeois consciousness. The very terms of opposition in traditional social work are formulated in the dualistic fashion which is characteristic of bourgeois society. For example, Marxists speak of 'liberating' and 'repressive' practice; feminists refer to 'sexist' and 'anti-sexist' attitudes. In short we are invited to reject traditional social work and accept radical social work totally. There is something very familiar about this. The debate in social work confronts us with the same false either/or option that has bedevilled mainstream western philosophy, at least since the time of Descartes. What is more, many radical assumptions seem to leap straight out of the pages of bourgeois dogma, for example the assumptions that the world can be improved through rational human intervention, that human beings are composed of common needs and desires which are distorted by uniform illusions ('class ideology'/patriarchy), that language is the servant of the user, and that it is viable to secure fixed and definite meanings in communication.

Now, there is no point in going the whole hog and rejecting all of these assumptions *tout court*. Rational intervention can lead to beneficial social change; needs and desires may be diverse, but some are less diverse than others; language can be used to make meaning, even if meaning is never entirely without ambiguity. All of this is obviously and demonstrably the case. But as we tried to show in Chapter 4, the kind of dynamics and subtleties in motion here are more complicated than most traditional or radical accounts allow. The main problem is that the received ideas of social work have not kept pace with the cultural and economic changes wrought by modernism. Received ideas of acceptance, self-determination and individualisation are drawn from the vocabulary of a very different type of society. The same is true of the received critique of traditional received ideas in social work, with its celebration of collectivism, equality, and commitment.

In this section we propose to discuss the two sides of received ideas which contribute most to their ineffectiveness under modernism: their historical remoteness and their abstraction. We shall refer to traditional and radical received ideas and practice and treat both as rooted in the consciousness of bourgeois society. We

170

shall not say much about the positive and enabling aspects of traditional and radical received ideas and practices, for we touched on these matters at the start of the chapter in our commentary on 'the social'.

Let us begin with the question of historical remoteness and take a concrete example to begin our discussion. The example refers to the condition of the poor in modern society and how social work relates to this issue. Traditional social work draws on its nineteenth-century legacy and continues to regard the poor as subjects for rehabilitation. Welfare is directed to the objects of maintaining survival and stimulating the poor to rise above their condition by entering the labour market as paid workers. Radical social work, at least in its progressive and contradictory Marxist incarnations, continues to impute revolutionary potential to the poor. Marx and Engels dubbed the unemployed as 'the reserve army of labour'. Progressive Marxist social workers look forward to the day when the poor will control the means of production as associated producers, jointly and directly determining collective welfare and the distribution of wealth. Yet what is the real condition of the poor in modern society?

They are, plainly, treated as surplus to the labour requirements of modern industry. The jobs they used to hold are now being done more cheaply and efficiently by machines. Micro-chip automated processes will probably accelerate and magnify this displacement of labour in the years up to 2000 and beyond. Furthermore, workers who are in secure jobs do not identify with the poor. They show no sign of enlisting 'the reserve army' for a final assault against capital. Indeed, ordinary working people harbour the most cynical suspicions about welfare claimants. Consider the jaundiced statement of a 28-year-old window cleaner who spoke as a delegate to the 1987 Conservative party conference:

> 'I object to seeing my hard-earned taxes supporting loafers who watch TV all day. Don't get me wrong, they are nice people but they are totally bone idle. Scroungers who turn work down when it is available must have their dole stopped.'
>
> (*Daily Mirror*, 7 October 1987)

Such sentiments are not uncommon among full-time workers today. However, it is unlikely that welfare payments will be stopped. The poor are primarily important in modern society not as a reserve army of labour but as the bottom rung in the market for consumer items. The dole provided for the recipient is paltry, but at least it keeps alive the dull compulsion to consume.

The example of the poor under modernism illustrates the deficiency of received ideas in traditional and radical social work to meet the felt needs of the people. The language is rich in descriptive vocabulary, but impoverished in an active vocabulary of what social workers and clients can do to amend their situation. Talk of rehabilitation or revolution seems inappropriate for the conditions and opportunities of life experienced by large numbers of the presently existing poor. The received language of need and desire, rights and obligations, is light-weight stuff when compared with the actual circumstances of modern society where the poor are increasingly treated as an outcast group.

The case of the poor by no means exhausts the range of relevant illustrations. For example, received ideas and received forms of intervention are also clearly inadequate in social work with racial minorities. Social work in Britain has failed to achieve anything other than sporadic and uneven communication with the needs and problems of black clients while for their part, black people have felt that the received ideas and received language of social work are remote from their everyday interests and problems. The feeling of remoteness can be measured in terms of the minuscule number of black people actually employed as social workers. It is estimated that there are no more than 300 qualified black social workers in Britain and only a handful occupy senior positions. Furthermore, in 1986 only one black person sat on the twenty-six-member Central Council for Education and Training in Social Work (*Guardian*, 29 December 1986).

Here again, a historical dimension is crucial for understanding this state of affairs. The received ideas and language of traditional social work were formulated in bourgeois society where the black population was negligible. Slavery and empire contributed degraded images of blacks as commodities or savages. For nineteenth-century white bourgeois society, civilising the black meant teaching an inferior person to be on good terms with his or her invincible simplicity. This racist stereotype was celebrated in popular culture, from school books to music-hall songs. The influx of black settlers into Britain after 1945 has done little to stem the ride of racism. People of Asian and West Indian origins are more likely than white people to be unemployed. Those in paid employment are more likely to be in jobs with lower pay and lower status than white people (see Brown 1984). Although neighbourhood development schemes in some inner-city areas do give black people the opportunity to have some influence in deter- 'mining local welfare provision, they are the exception to the rule. In general, black people do not play a significant part in planning and administering welfare services. The invisibility of the black client in traditional social policy and traditional social work is mirrored in radical theory. The dilemmas and hazards of organis- ing class action in a multiracial society with a substantial black underclass have hardly even been considered in most Marxist accounts of social transformation. The progressive and contradic- tory Marxist social worker intent on applying Marxist principles in modern society faces the same basic problem as his or her traditional counterpart: the received language and the received ideas seem incapable of providing helpful or convincing solutions to the problems which they actually encounter.

In contrast to Marxism, feminist writers and social workers have adopted a more realistic attitude to the question of race. In large part this reflects the greater sensitivity of feminism to the varieties of power in modern society and, in particular, to the symbolic representation of exploitation, deprivation, and repres- sion through language. However, feminists have not escaped the problems of pluralism, division, and conflict. 'Black feminists', remarks Wilson with Weir (1986: 103) 'have criticised as racist the attempt by white feminists to erect a unitary theory of women's oppression.'

Having considered the examples of the poor and ethnic minorities, we are perhaps now in a better position to understand the relation between received ideas, modernism, and social work. The roots of traditional and radical received ideas are firmly embedded in bourgeois society. The seeds were planted as a result of the bourgeois demands for the rational administration of the poor. The bourgeoisie required a form of social work in which there was a clear division between the duties of the social worker and the needs of the client. Problems were regarded as having fixed and definite solutions. Adult 'normality' was identified with a state of propertied, waged existence in which marital and family responsibilities were scrupulously obeyed. Social workers enour- aged the poor to aspire to this state of affairs in their own lives. In effect, all classes were required to capitulate to the prosaic ideal of bourgeois lifestyle.

It is fruitless to argue that social work has abandoned the

demand for the rational administration of the client. However, it is pursued in dramatically altered social conditions. Under modernism, not only administration, but rationality itself is regarded with scepticism. The possibilities of fixed and definite meaning, the objective classification of social need, the determination of necessary services is openly, and sometimes violently, questioned. The professional language of care is attacked as 'control talk'. The attempt to build whole relationships and whole services is seen as a suspect, quaint ambition. Attachments and commitments in modern life are portrayed as overwhelmingly unstable and fragmentary. Intervention into another person's life, or the life of society, drags with it a tangle of unforeseen and unplanned consequences.

By considering the historical origins of received ideas, a clearer picture of the problems that social workers face in communicating and acting with clients emerges. However, as we indicated in the opening lines of this section, understanding the deficiencies of received ideas in modern social work is not simply a matter of paying more attention to history. The question of the abstraction of received ideas is also crucial. By abstraction we mean a form of communication which is based in general principles and general cases. We argued in Chapter 1 that the key received ideas in traditional social work are abstractions – ideas like 'trust', 'respect', 'acceptance', 'confidentiality', etc. The main problem is that the demands that clients bring to social workers are not standardised or general but unique and concrete. Social workers build their theories and policies around the problems of 'Humanity'. However, social workers do not deal with 'Humanity', they deal with the problems of particular human beings in a particular complex of relations with nature, history and themselves. Because received ideas apply to the problems of the average caseload and the normal social worker, they tend to stereotype the actually existing conditions which the social worker encounters. For example, the social worker 'knows' the problems of an unemployed person, a person of no fixed abode, or an abused child before coming into contact with real individuals. Similarly, social workers 'know' what is in the best interests of their clients, regardless of whether this corresponds to the clients' own view of what is in their best interests.

Now, we are fully aware that general, transferable knowledge is indispensable. Without it, social workers would be forced to invent social work from scratch every time they started work with a new client. However, the move from the specific to the general, and vice versa, is not always examined with sufficient critical awareness. To be sure, under social conditions where social work departments are under-staffed and required by management to achieve set performance targets, the slide into reification – the turning of the client into a thing – is accomplished only too easily. Under such conditions, where many urgent demands are made on clients, the social worker recites 'causes' and 'solutions' instead of thinking; instead of providing relevant help, the administration of care clicks into motion and follows its time-honoured course. All too often the client is transformed from an individual with a unique biography, and hence a unique set of needs, into a mere object of received thought and administration.

Conclusion: what is to be done?

Giving the client hope for a better future is a common feature of traditional and radical social work. Yet the future is reliant upon the past and the present. In this chapter we have argued that the past of social work was shaped by the certainties of bourgeois society. In the rule-governed ideology of the bourgeois world, the social worker knew what was best for the client, and the best interests of the client were assumed to coincide with the best interests of society. Things are very different today. The modern social worker labours in a climate of violent, unaccustomed, and changing uncertainties. Thus, it can no longer be assumed that the 'normal' domestic unit in society is the nuclear family in which the husband is the main breadwinner and the wife is the home-maker. However, as we showed in Chapter 3, social workers oper-ate in a framework of social policy on women and the family which perpetuates exactly the opposite received ideas. Similarly, it can no longer be assumed that the client will be employed full-time or part-time in a single trade or occupation. Given the realities of the employment market in depressed areas, social workers may be forced to collude with clients who participate in the infor-mal economy as well as claiming unemployment and welfare benefit. For the alternative may be to plunge the client and depen-dent family into a life which is below the poverty line. Similar pressures impinge upon social workers who work with black clients and deal with legislation, local employment markets, and neighbourhoods which reinforce racial discrimination. The social worker must struggle to reconcile interests which may be objectively irreconcilable and produce solutions for social problems which exist in a molten, changeable condition.

The situation of uncertainty is compounded by the enormous range of conflicting theories of social problems and social work intervention that the social worker can choose from. As we remarked earlier in the chapter, the inevitable consequence of the creation of 'the social' as an area of full-time, legitimate, practice and enquiry was the production of knowledge and theories on the nature of the social. This has left the social worker with a rich but confusing legacy of received ideas. It is not simply that traditional and radical social workers hold different positions on the nature of society, social problems, and the social work task. A major argument of our book has been that within these traditions there are serious and violent divisions. For example, our discussion of progressive Marxists and radical separatist feminists indicates that they oppose traditional social work but propagate very different theories of affirmative action. Given these divisions, the immediate and medium-term prospect of consensus and collective action between them is dim. When the full range of dissonance within radical social work described in this book is taken into account, the prospect seems to dwindle into insignificance. The social worker is left in a quandary. 'Professionalism is breaking up,' writes Pearson (1975: 62), 'and yet, at the same time, there is abroad a sense of gloom and dejection: where to turn, what to do, how to help?'

Feelings of gloom, dejection, and anxiety are, of course, perfectly consistent with our description of modernism. They are the corollaries of that form of consciousness which views itself and the world as dynamic, fragmentary, many-sided, and discontinuous. We should not be surprised that these feelings are common among social workers. After all, they exist in extreme and sometimes chronic form among clients. Social workers deal regularly with depressed people; people who feel that their lives have been stilled by arbitrary tragedy or random misfortune. In such circumstances, talk, one of the most powerful weapons of the social worker, may seem oppressive. Society requires the social worker to offer solutions to personal problems in conditions where the causes of problems are often obscure and the stability of situations is not guaranteed. What is more, society also requires the social worker to be accountable. The state which employs the social worker also monitors work done and has the power to challenge decisions and discipline actions. In short, there are good material reasons why social workers should feel anxious, gloomy, confused, and dejected in their work.

However, to dwell only on the negative features of social work and to link them to the negative characteristics of modernism is to give a one-sided picture. Dynamism may be unsettling, but it can also be challenging and exciting. Similarly, to think of our actions as many-sided and our efforts as fragmentary, discontinuous, and unstable may fuel our uncertainties, but it can also produce more tolerance with respect to our judgements of our efforts and the conduct of others. Modernism shakes the sediment in the glass and gives social workers opportunities to break free from encrusted, authoritarian influences. It can produce fundamental learning experiences for social workers, and inspire new forms of creativity in managing caseloads and improving the well-being of clients.

Change does not occur automatically. If social workers are to contribute to relevant systems of care they must take critical stock of the established system of welfare provision. Historically speaking, the welfare state has assumed a donatory character which embodies a strong distinction between the provider of services (the social worker) and the recipient (the client). The received ideas and language of social work bear the hallmark of this character. Social workers have pursued the ideology of 'service to others' and 'giving rather than receiving'. They have insisted on the need to practise acceptance and trust in their relations with clients. Yet they have preserved and refined legal powers which enable them to define some forms of social behaviour as unacceptable and some people as untrustworthy. None of this has rid social work of its hierarchical and bureaucratic image. On the contrary, social workers are regularly criticised for being remote from the real needs of people. As we have argued again and again in this book the received ideas and language of social work are frequently singled out as symbols of what is wrong with social work. Even a liberal paper like the *Guardian* recently commented in an article entitled 'A case of bad treatment for social work':

> [Social workers] are their own worst enemies in refusing to speak in plain English and instead taking refuge behind an incomprehensible sociological jargon which at best conceals muddled and woolly thinking. The popular image of the hairy leftie who spouts sociobabble is not altogether a myth.
>
> (*Guardian*, 11 December 1987)

To understand how our needs and obligations compare and differ we must speak in open and relevant ways. We want to see a welfare system which takes the unique needs of clients seriously; and a form of social work that handles issues of gender, class, race, and handicap positively, i.e. not as a 'social problem'. In our view this requires a move away from a *donatory* to *participatory* form of care.

In saying this we are fully aware that community workers have made many significant experiments in decentralising power (see Beresford and Croft 1986). The development of participation in decision-making is a key theme in many community programmes. Community workers aim to help 'users and others in the community to take up more responsibility for neighbourhood functions such as socialisation, social control and mutual support, and achieving the resources to do this' (Henderson and Thomas 1985: 18). Community work has given ordinary people the experience of managing their own affairs directly. Nevertheless, it is based on inherent limitations. For one thing, the spread of community schemes is rather uneven. There is little consistency in local political support throughout the country. So some areas have highly developed schemes, while others have no real community participation to speak of. A related point is perhaps more important. Community work is notorious for being precariously funded. Workers in some schemes do not know what they will receive from year to year or, in some cases, from month to month. This restricts planning capacities and damages the stability of participation. Community workers are too often forced to divert their energies from vital educational and developmental functions to crisis management. We have already considered another limitation of community work in this chapter: that is, the implausible, romantic ideals of belonging and mutual responsibility that the architects of community care often claim for their programmes. It is important to be sober in our assessments of what participatory welfare can achieve and not burden it with unrealistic expectations.

Our position is that community work has produced vital experience of participatory welfare. However, the experience must be taken much further in social work and funded adequately. We have written elsewhere of the promise and form of decentralisation in social work (see Rojek, Peacock, and Collins 1989, especially Chapters 4 and 8). We do not intend to duplicate our remarks in detail here. Even so, since we have raised the question of what is to be done in social work, we cannot let the occasion pass without some comments on the forms of participation that we envisage. With the limited nature of our discussion understood, let us make the following points.

The move to participatory systems of social work aims to achieve the maximum participation of social workers, representatives of the community, and clients in the administration and planning of local welfare services. This aim is inspired by the belief that the most neglected resources in the current system are the ideas and experience of clients, members of the community, basic grade workers, social work assistants, home-makers, home helps, cleaning and maintenance staff, etc. The current hierarchical system allows them to express their ideas and experience in an *ad hoc* way. However, it does not give these crucial workers direct participation and thus offers no formal way of translating their ideas and experience into policy. Not only does this breed resentment and negativism, it also squanders one of the most crucial resources in providing relevant services: the talents and energies of people on the spot.

Participatory management will need to retain the posts of Area Manager, Officer in Charge, and Head of Home, for all organisations require a symbolic head. However, the posts should be open to regular and free elections. No incumbent should be permitted to serve more than two consecutive terms of office. The head of the organisation should be charged with the task of executing the decisions of the participatory board. Participatory boards should be self-managing units composed of representatives from social work, the community, and client collectives. Like the head position, no representative should be permitted to serve for more than two consecutive terms. The purpose of the participatory board will be to provide flexible and relevant systems of care for local needs. The board will receive an annual income from central government and determine the allocation of resources between pay, education, development, transport, maintenance, etc. Each board will be bound by a constitution of participation which sets out the rights and responsibilities of the system. The constitution should take account of local traditions and local needs and be regularly assessed for its relevance.

No system of management and no person is without fault. In order to protect the participatory boards from abuses such as personality cults or fraud, the professional associations and trade unions in social work, such as BASW and NALGO, should be

179

retained. The purposes of these organisations should be to supervise elections, arrange for disciplinary hearings to be conducted fairly, and disseminate information.

Anyone who has understood our arguments about received ideas on social work and modernism correctly will see that participatory systems of management will not put an end to ambiguity. Carers will still argue about the meaning of needs, the obligations of welfare agencies, the distribution of resources, etc. On the other hand, participation will certainly enable social workers, clients, and members of the community to be exposed in concrete ways to the diversity of values and needs in society. It will also give them first-hand knowledge of the capacities of the welfare services to meet values and needs. Clients and social workers are skilled and talented people. Their skills and talents must be used, not by fiat but by partnership, to build systems of care which are more relevant to felt needs. It is not enough to let clients, basic grade workers, and ancillary staff speak. They must be given real powers to make their words count in the planning and administration of care.

Notes

2 The Marxist alternative

1 See, in particular, Lemert (1967); Douglas (1967, 1970); Kitsuse (1962); Matza (1964, 1969).

2 In general Marxist and neo-Marxist commentators on social work in the west have shown a puzzling disregard for the experience of social work in 'the presently existing socialist societies'. A vital comparative dimension in understanding social work in modern industrial society is therefore missing. There is an urgent need for a comparative study of the variations in welfare organisation and social work training within the Soviet bloc (e.g. comparing the system in a more 'liberal' Socialist country like Hungary with more 'authoritarian' countries in the Warsaw Pact group, such as Poland and the USSR). Furthermore, it would be fascinating to know what social workers mean by received ideas like 'trust', 'confidentiality', 'acceptance', 'need', 'liberation', 'consciousness-raising', etc., in the context of the party state structure.

3 See, in particular, Thompson (1963); Hill (1961, 1975); Hobsbawm (1959, 1969); Hilton (1969).

4 See, in particular, Adorno and Horkheimer (1979); Adorno (1973); Horkheimer (1974); Della Volpe (1960); Barthes (1957): Williams (1961, 1976).

5 Engels delivered the oration at Highgate Cemetery, London, on 17 March 1883. The text is reproduced in Marx and Engels (1968: 429-30).

6 Note the abstraction of keywords like 'community', 'consciousness', 'awareness', and 'authority' in this passage. Without any concrete reference to historical-material conditions, such words admit a huge range of conflicting meanings. We return to this point in Chapter 5.

7 The schema appeared in slightly amended form in Rojek (1985, 1986).

3 Women, social work, and feminism

1 CCETSW's proposals for a unified training (QDSW) are under review at the time of writing.

4 Social work, humanism, and discourse analysis

1 Cited by Spivak in her Preface to Derrida (1977: xxii).
2 Cited by Eagleton (1983:201)
3 The term 'remissive culture' was coined by Carroll (1985).

5 'The social' in social work

1 This is, of course, the stuff of current right-wing rhetoric. Family and community care is in fact a code-word for 'voluntary care', i.e.

unpaid work done for dependants in the privacy of the home, usually by women (wives, mothers, daughters). The New Right is strongly attracted to voluntary care as a low-cost option to expand the management of welfare in the years up to 2000 and beyond. 'Caring capitalism', in this context, really means asking women to do more for less.

References

Adorno, T.W. (1973) *The Jargon of Authenticity*, London: Routledge & Kegan Paul.

Adorno, T.W. and Horkheimer, M. (1979) *Dialectic of Enlightenment*, London: Verso (first published 1944).

Althusser, L. (1971) *Lenin, Philosophy and Other Essays*, London: New Left Books.

Anderson, P. (1983) *In the Tracks of Historical Materialism*, London: Verso.

Atherton, J.S. (1986) *Professional Supervision in Group Care*, London: Tavistock.

Bailey, R. and Brake, M. (1975) (eds.) *Radical Social Work*, London: Edward Arnold.

Barclay Report (1982) *Social Workers, their Roles and Tasks*, London: Bedford Square Press.

Barker, H. (1986) 'Restructuring sisterhood: a critical look at "process" in feminist organising and community work', *Critical Social Policy* 6(1): 80-91.

Barr, E. (1974) 'Understanding Lacan', in L. Goldberger, (ed.) *Psychoanalysis and Contemporary Science*, New York: International University Press.

Barrett, M. (1986) *Women's Oppression Today*, London: Verso.

Barrett, M. and McIntosh, M. (1982) *The Anti-Social Family*, London: Verso.

Barthes, R. (1957) *Mythologies*, St Albans: Paladin.

BASW (1975) 'A code of ethics for social work', in D. Watson (ed.) (1985) *A Code of Ethics for Social Work: The Second Step*, London: Routledge & Kegan Paul.

BASW (1980) *Clients Are Fellow Citizens*, Birmingham: British Association of Social Workers.

BASW (1986) *Annual Review 1985-86*, Birmingham: British Association of Social Workers.

Bean, P., Ferris, J., and Whynes, D. (1985) *In Defence of Welfare*, London: Tavistock.

Becker, H.S. (1963) *Outsiders*, New York: Free Press.

Beecher, S. (1986) 'A gender critique of family therapy' in H. Marchant and B. Wearing (eds.) *Gender Reclaimed: Women in Social Work*, Sydney: Hale & Iremonger.

Beer, S. (1982) *Britain Against Itself: the Political Contradictions of Collectivism*, London: Faber & Faber.

Beresford, P. and Croft, S. (1986) *Whose Welfare?*, Brighton: Louis Cohen Urban Studies Centre.

Berger, P. and Luckman, J.T. (1967) *The Social Construction of Reality*, London: Allen Lane.

Bernard, J. (1972) *The Future of Marriage*, Harmondsworth: Penguin.

Beveridge, W. (1942) *Social Insurance and Allied Services*, London: HMSO.

Biestek, F.P. (1961) *The Casework Relationship*, London: Allen & Unwin.

Biestek, F.P. and Gehrig, C. (1978) *Client Self-Determination, A Fifty-year History*, Chicago: Soyola University Press.

Bird, J. (1982) 'Jacques Lacan – the French Freud?', *Radical Philosophy* 30: 7-13.

183

References

Birmingham Women and Social Work Group 81 (1985) 'Women and social work in Birmingham', in E. Brook and A. Davis *Women, the Family and Social Work*, London: Tavistock.

Bloch, E. (1986) *The Principle of Hope* (3 vols), Oxford: Blackwell.

Bolger, S., Corrigan, P., Docking, J., and Frost, N. (1981) *Towards Social Welfare Work*, London: Macmillan.

Bosanquet, B. (1901) 'The meaning of social work', *International Journal of Ethics* 11(3).

Brager, G. and Barr, S. (1967) 'Perceptions and reality, the poor man's view of social services', in G. Brager, and F.P. Purcell (eds.) *Community Action Against Poverty*, New Haven, Conn.: College & University Press.

Brandon, D. and Jordan, B. (eds.) (1979) *Creative Social Work*, Oxford: Blackwell.

Brenton, M. and Jones, C. (1985) *The Yearbook of Social Policy in Britain 1984-85*, London: Routledge & Kegan Paul.

Brewer, C. and Lait, J. (1980) *Can Social Work Survive?*, London: Temple Smith.

Briar, S. (1968) 'The casework predicament', *Social Work* 13(1).

Brook, E. and Davis, A. (1985) *Women, the Family and Social Work*, London: Tavistock.

Brown, C. (1984) *Black and White Britain: 3rd PSI Survey*, London: Heinemann.

Bucker, H.R. and Stelling, J. (1977) *Becoming a Professional*, London: Sage.

Burden, D. and Gottlieb, N. (1987) *The Woman Client*, London: Tavistock.

Carnegie, A. (1896) 'How I served my apprenticeship as a businessman', *The Youth's Companion*, 23 April 1896.

Carroll, J. (1985) *Guilt: the Grey Eminence behind Character, History and Culture*, London: Routledge & Kegan Paul.

CCETSW (1976) *Values in Social Work*, London: Central Council for Education and Training in Social Work.

Chodrow, N. (1978) *The Reproduction of Mothering*, Los Angeles: University of California Press.

Clark, C. with Asquith, S. (1985) *Social Work and Social Philosophy*, London: Routledge & Kegan Paul.

Cohen, S. (1972) *Folk Devils and Moral Panics*, London: Macgibbon & Kee.

Cohen, S. (1975) 'It's all right for you to talk: political and sociological manifestos for social work action', in R. Bailey and M. Brake (eds.) *Radical Social Work*, London: Edward Arnold.

Cohen, S. (1985) *Visions of Social Control*, Oxford: Polity.

Corrigan, P. and Leonard, P. (1978) *Social Work Practice under Capitalism*, London: Macmillan.

Corrigan, P. and Sayer, D. (1985) *The Great Arch: English State Formation as Cultural Revolution*, Oxford: Blackwell.

Coward, R. (1978) 'Sexual liberation and the family', *M/F* 1.

Croft, S. (1986) 'Women, caring and recasting of need – a feminist appraisal', *Critical Social Policy* 13: 23-39.

Dale, J. and Foster, P. (1986) *Feminists and State Welfare*, London: Routledge & Kegan Paul.

Davies, M. (1981) *The Essential Social Worker*, London: Heinemann.

Davies, M. and Knopf, A. (1973) *Social Enquiry Reports and Probation Service*, London: Home Office Research Studies, HMSO.

References

Day, P. (1981) *Social Work and Social Control*, London: Tavistock.

Deacon, R. and Bartley, M. (1975) 'Becoming a social worker', in H. Jones (ed.) *Towards a New Social Work*, London: Routledge & Kegan Paul

Della Volpe, G. (1960) *Critique of Taste*, London: New Left Books.

Densmore, D. (1969) 'On sisterhood. No more fun and games', *A Journal of Female Liberation*, Issue 2, Cambridge, Mass.

Derrida, J. (1977) *Of Grammatology*, trans. G.K. Spivak, Baltimore: Johns Hopkins Press.

Derrida, J. (1981) *Positions*, New York: Athlone Press.

Dingwall, R. (1977) *The Social Organisation of Health Visitor Training*, London: Croom Helm.

Donzelot, J. (1979) *The Policing of Families*, London: Hutchinson.

Dorwick, C. (1983) 'Strange meeting: Marxism, psychoanalysis and social work', *British Journal of Social Work* 13(1): 1-18.

Douglas, J.D. (1967) *The Social Meanings of Suicide*, Princeton, NJ: Princeton University Press.

Douglas, J.D. (1970) *Deviance and Respectability: the Social Construction of Moral Meanings*, New York: Basic Books.

Douglas, T. (1979) *Group Processes in Social Work*, New York: Wiley.

Doyal, L. and Gough, I. (1984) 'A theory of human needs', *Critical Social Policy* 10: 6-38.

Dunbar, R. (1970) 'Female liberation as the basis for social revolution', in R. Morgan (ed.) *Sisterhood Is Powerful*, New York: Random House.

Eagleton, T. (1983) *Literary Theory*, Oxford: Blackwell.

Edelman, M. (1977) *Political Language: Words that Succeed and Policies that Fail*, New York: Academic Press.

Eisenstein, Z. (1979) *The Radical Future of Liberal Feminism*, New York: Longman.

Eisenstein, Z. (1981) 'Reform and/or Revolution: towards a united women's movement', in L. Sargent (ed.) *Women and Revolution*, London: Pluto.

Engels, F. (1972) *The Origin of the Family, Private Property and the State*, New York: Pathfinder.

Engels, F. (1973) *The Condition of the Working Class in England*, Moscow: Progress Publishers.

Equal Opportunities Commission (1984) *Carers and Services: a Comparison of Men and Women Caring for Dependent Elderly People*, Manchester: EOC.

Finch, J. and Groves, D. (1980) 'Community care and the family: a case for equal opportunities', *Journal of Social Policy* 9 (4): 487-511.

Finch J. and Groves, D. (1983) *A Labour of Love: Women, Work and Caring*, London: Routledge & Kegan Paul.

Firestone, S. (1971) *The Dialectic of Sex*, New York: Bantam.

Fischer, J. (1976) *The Effectiveness of Social Casework*, Ill.: Charles C. Thomas.

Flew, A. (1985) 'Do-gooders doing no good?' in M. Brenton, and C. Jones (eds.) *The Yearbook of Social Policy in London 1984-85*, London: Routledge & Kegan Paul.

Freire, P. (1970) *Pedagogy of the Oppressed*, Harmondsworth: Penguin.

Freud, S. (1979) *Civilisation and its Discontents*, London: Hogarth.

References

Friedan, B. (1965) *The Feminine Mystique*, Harmondsworth: Penguin.

Friedman, M. and Friedman, R. (1980) *Free To Choose*, Harmondsworth: Penguin.

Folkard, M.S. (1974) *IMPACT: Intensive Matched Probation and After-Care Treatment*, London: HMSO.

Foucault, M. (1975) *Discipline and Punish*, Harmondsworth: Penguin.

Foucault, M. (1980) *Power/Knowledge* (ed.) C. Gibson, Brighton: Harvester.

Foucault, M. (1981) 'Questions of method: an interview with Michel Foucault', *Ideology and Consciousness* 8: 3-14.

Fox, A. (1974) *Beyond Contract: Work, Power and Trust Relations*, London: Faber.

Galper, J. (1975) *The Politics of Social Service*, New York: Prentice Hall.

Gans, H. (1968) 'Urban poverty and social planning', in P. Lazarsfeld *et al.* (eds.) *The Uses of Urban Sociology*, London: Weidenfeld.

Garrett, A. (1949) 'The worker client relationship', *American Journal of Orthopsychiatry* 19(2).

Ginsburg, N. (1979) *Class, Capital and Social Policy*, London: Macmillan.

Goldstein, H. (1981) *Social Learning and Change*, London: Tavistock.

Goode, W. (1957) 'Community with a community: the professions', *American Sociological Review* 22.

Gorz, A. (1982) *Farewell to the Working Class*, London: Pluto.

Gough, I. (1979) *The Political Economy of the Welfare State*, London: Macmillan.

Guettel, C. (1974) *Marxism and Feminism*, Toronto: The Women's Press.

Hale, J. (1983) 'Feminism and social work practice', in B. Jordan and N. Parton (eds.) *Political Dimensions of Social Work*, Oxford: Blackwell.

Hamner, J. and Statham, D. (1987) 'Commonalities and diversities reassessed' *Social Work Today*, 16 February 1987: 13.

Hamner, J. and Statham, D. (1988) *Women and Social Work: Women Centred Practice*, London: Macmillan/BASW.

Hardiker, P. (1977) 'Social work ideologies in the probation service', *British Journal of Social Work* 7(2): 131-54.

Harris, R. and Seldon, A. (1979) *Over-Ruled on Welfare*, London: Institute of Economic Affairs.

Hearn, J. (1985) 'Patriarchy, professionalisation and the semi-professions', in C. Ungerson (ed.) *Women and Social Policy*, London: Macmillan.

Hebdige, D. (1979) *Subculture: the Meaning of Style*, London: Methuen.

Henderson, P. and Thomas, D. (1985) 'Out into the community', *Community Care* 573: 17-19.

Heraud, B. (1970) *Sociology and Social Work*, Oxford: Pergamon.

Heraud, B. (1981) *Training for Uncertainty: a Sociological Approach to Social Work*, London: Routledge & Kegan Paul.

Hill, C. (1961) *The Century of Revolution 1605-1714*, Edinburgh: Nelson.

Hill, C. (1975) *The World Turned Upside Down*, Harmondsworth: Penguin.

Hill, O. (1893) 'Trained workers for the poor', *Nineteenth Century* January 1893.

Hilton, R. (1969) *Decline of Serfdom in England*, London: Macmillan.

Hilton, R. (1976) (ed.) *The Transition from Feudalism to Capitalism*, London: New Left Books.

References

Himmelfarb, G. (1984) *The Idea of Poverty*, London: Faber.

Hindess, B. (1986) *Freedom, Equality and the Market*, London: Tavistock.

HMSO (1942) 'Report on the social insurance and allied services' (Beveridge Report) Cmnd 64 04, London: HMSO.

HMSO (1983) *Social Trends* 13, London: HMSO.

HMSO (1987) *Social Trends* 17, London: HMSO.

Hobsbawm, E. (1959) *Primitive Rebels*, Manchester: Manchester University Press.

Hobsbawm, E. (1969) *Labouring Men*, London: Weidenfeld & Nicolson.

Hollis, F. (1952) 'Principles and assumptions underlying casework practice', address given at Bedford College, London.

Hollis, F. (1969) *Casework, a Psychosocial Therapy*, New York: Random House.

Horkheimer, M. (1974) *Eclipse of Reason*, New York: Continuum.

Horney, K. (1967) *Feminine Psychology*, New York: Morton.

Hudson, A. (1983) 'The welfare state and adolescent femininity', *Youth and Policy* 2(1): 5-13.

Hughes, E. (1958) *Men and their Work*, Chicago: Free Press.

Hugman, B. (1977) *Act Natural*, London: Bedford Square Press.

Ignatieff, M. (1984) *The Needs of Strangers*, London: Chatto & Windus.

Irvine, E.E. (1956) 'Transference and reality in the casework relationship', *British Journal of Psychiatric Social Work* 3 (4).

Jack, R. (1987) 'Women in care', *Social Services Insight*, 20 March 1987: 18-20.

Johnson, P. (1982) 'Family Reunion', *Observer*, 10 October 1982.

Jones, C. (1983) *State Social Work and the Working Class*, London: Macmillan.

Jones, H. (1975) (ed.) *Towards a New Social Work*, London: Routledge & Kegan Paul.

Kern, S. (1983) *The Culture of Time and Space 1880-1918*, London: Weidenfeld and Nicolson.

Kitsuse, J. (1962) 'Social reaction to deviant behaviour: problems of theory and method', *Social Problems* 9 (Winter): 247-56.

Kovel, J. (1981) *A Complete Guide to Theory*, Harmondsworth: Penguin.

Lacan, J. (1977) *Ecrits*, London: Tavistock.

Langan, M. (1985) 'The unitary approach: a feminist critique', in E. Brook and A. Davis (eds.) *Women, the Family and Social Work*, London: Tavistock.

Lasch, C. (1980) *The Culture of Narcissism*, London: Abacus.

Lemert, E.M. (1967) *Human Deviance, Social Problems and State Control*, New York: Prentice Hall.

Leonard, P. (1984) *Personality and Ideology*, London: Macmillan.

Local Government Operational Research Unit (1984) *Developing the Neglected Resource: an Action Report*, London: RIPA Services Ltd.

Local Government Training Board (1986) 'Survey of manpower and qualifications within social service departments in England and Wales, and Social Work Departments in Scotland', London: LGTB.

Loch, F.S. (1906) *Introduction to Annual Charities Register*, 15th edn., London: Longman.

Lowe, D. (1982) *History of Bourgeois Perception*, Brighton: Harvester.

187

References

McDermott, C. (1975) *Self Determination in Social Work*, London: Routledge & Kegan Paul.

McDonough, R. and Harrison, (1978) 'Patriarchy and relations of production, in A. Kuhn and A. Wolpe (eds.) *Feminism and Materialism*, London: Routledge & Kegan Paul.

Maluccio, A.N. and Marlow, D.W. (1974) 'The case for the contract', *Social Work* (USA) 13(3).

Marchant, H. (1986) 'Gender systems thinking and radical social work', in H. Marchant and B. Wearing (eds.) *Gender Reclaimed: Women in Social Work*, Sydney: Hale & Iremonger.

Marchant, H. and Wearing, B. (1986) (eds.) *Gender Reclaimed: Women in Social Work*, Sydney: Hale & Iremonger.

Marcuse (1964) *One Dimensional Man*, London: Sphere.

Marx, K. (1964) *The Economic and Philosophical Manuscripts of 1844*, New York: International Publishers.

Marx, K. (1977) *Capital, Vol.1*, London: Lawrence & Wishart.

Marx, K. and Engels, F. (1968) *Selected Works in One Volume*, London: Lawrence & Wishart.

Marx, K. and Engels, F. (1970) *The German Ideology*, London: Lawrence & Wishart.

Matza, D. (1964) *Delinquency and Drift*, New York: Wiley.

Matza, D. (1969) *Becoming Deviant*, New York: Prentice Hall.

Mayo, M. (1977) *Women in the Community*, London: Routledge & Kegan Paul.

Means, R. (1979) 'Which way for radical social work?', *British Journal of Social Work* 19(1): 15-28.

Miles, J. (1981) 'Sexism in social work', *Social Work Today* 13(1): 14-15.

Miller, J.B. (1973) *Psychoanalysis and Women*, Harmondsworth: Penguin.

Millett, K. (1970) *Sexual Politics*, New York: Doubleday.

Mitchell, J. (1971) *Woman's Estate*, Harmondsworth: Penguin.

Mitchell, J. (1974) *Psychoanalysis and Feminism*, London: Allen Lane.

Molyneux, M. (1984) 'Mobilisation without emancipation', *Critical Social Policy* 10: 59-75.

Mullen, E. and Dumpson, S. (1972) *Evaluation of Social Intervention*, New York: Josey Bass.

Müller, W. and Neusüss, C. (1978) 'The "welfare-state illusion" and the contradictions between wage-labour and capital', in J. Holloway and S. Piciotto (eds.) *State and Capital*, London: Edward Arnold.

NASW (1958) 'Working definition of social work practice', *Social Work* 3 (April): 5-9.

NASW (1980) *Code of Ethics of the National Association of Social Workers*, Washington DC.

New, C. and David, M. (1985) *For the Sake of the Children: Making Child Care More than Women's Business*, Harmondsworth: Penguin.

Nursten, J. (1974) *Process of Casework*, London: Pitman.

Oakley, A. (1987) 'The woman's place', *New Society*, 16 March 1987.

Parkinson, G. (1977) 'I give them money', in M. Fitzgerald, P. Halmos, J. Muncie, and D. Zedlin (eds.) *Welfare in Action*, London: Routledge & Kegan Paul.

Parry, N., Rustin, M., and Satyamurti, C. (1979) *Social Work, Welfare and the State*, London: Edward Arnold.

Pascall, G. (1986) *Social Policy: a Feminist Analysis*, London: Tavistock.

Pearson, G. (1975a) 'Making social workers: bad promises and good omens', in R. Bailey and M. Brake (eds.) *Radical Social Work*, London: Edward Arnold.

Pearson, G. (1975b) 'The politics of uncertainity: a study in the socialisation of the social worker', in H. Jones (ed.) *Towards a New Social Work*, London: Routledge & Kegan Paul.

Perlman, H. (1957) *Social Casework*, Chicago: University of Chicago Press.

Phillipson, C. (1982) *Capitalism and the Construction of Old Age*, London: Macmillan.

Philp, M. (1979) 'Notes on the form of knowledge in social work', *Sociological Review* 27(1): 83-111.

Pincus, A. and Minahan, A. (1973) *Social Work Practice: Model and Method*, Itasca, Ill.: Peacock Press.

Pincus, A. and Minahan, A. (1977) 'A Model for Social Work Practice', in H. Specht and A. Vickery (eds.) *Integrating Social Work Methods*, London: Allen & Unwin.

Plant, R. (1970) *Social Work and Moral Theory in Casework*, London: Routledge & Kegan Paul.

Pollak, O. (1960) 'Differential diagnosis and treatment of character disturbances', *Social Casework* (December).

Poulantzas, N. (1975) 'The new petty Bourgeoisie' in A. Hunt (ed.) *Class and Structure*, London: Lawrence & Wishart.

Pritchard, C. and Taylor, R. (1978) *Social Work: Reform or Revolution?*, London: Routledge & Kegan Paul.

Psathas, G. (1972) 'Ethnomethods and phenomenology', in V.G. Manis and B.N. Meltzer (eds.) *Symbolic Interaction: a Reader in Social Psychology*, Boston: Allyn & Beacon.

Ragg, N. (1977) *People Not Cases*, London: Routledge & Kegan Paul.

Rees, S. (1978) *Social Work Face To Face*, London: Edward Arnold.

Rees, S. and Wallace, A. (1982) *Verdicts on Social Work*, London: Edward Arnold.

Reid, W. (1978) *The Task Centred System*, New York: Columbia University Press.

Rhodes, M. (1986) *Ethical Dilemmas in Social Work Practice*, London: Routledge & Kegan Paul.

Richan, C. and Mendelsohn, F.R. (1973) *Social Work: the Unloved Profession*, New York: Franklin Watts.

Richmond, M. (1917) *Social Diagnosis*, New York: Russell Sage.

Robinson, T. (1978) *In Worlds Apart*, London: Bedford Square Press.

Rogers, C. (1951) *Client Centred Therapy*, Boston: Houghton & Mifflin.

Rojek, C. (1985) 'The "transition" problem in Marxist social work', in M. Brenton and C. Jones (eds.) *The Yearbook of Social Policy in Britain 1984-85*, London: Routledge & Kegan Paul.

Rojek, C. (1986) 'The "subject" in social work', *British Journal of Social Work* 16: 65-77.

Rojek, C. and Collins, S.A. (1987) 'Contract or con trick?' *British Journal of Social Work* 17: 199-211.

Rojek, C., Peacock, G. and Collins, S. (1989) (eds.) *The Haunt of Misery*, London: Routledge.

References

Rossi, A. (1972) 'Sex equality: the beginnings of ideology', in C. Safilios-Rothschild (ed.) *Towards a Sociology of Women*, Lexington: Xerox.

Rowbotham, S. (1973) *Women's Consciousness, Man's World*, Harmondsworth: Penguin.

St John-Brooks, C. (1987) 'A woman's place', *New Society* 79(1262).

Satyamurti, C. (1979) *Occupational Survival*, Oxford: Blackwell.

Saussure, F. de (1974) *Course in General Linguistics*, London: Fontana.

Sayers, J. (1982) *Biological Politics: Feminist and Anti-Feminist Perspectives*, London: Tavistock.

Sayers, S. (1985) *Reality and Reason*, Oxford: Blackwell.

Scott, W.R. (1969) 'Professional employees in a bureaucratic structure: social work', in A. Etzioni (ed.) *The Semi-Professions and their Organisations*, New York: Free Press.

Sedgwick, P. (1982) *Psychopolitics*, London: Pluto.

Sennett, R. (1977) *The Fall of Public Man*, London: Faber.

Simpkin, M. (1979) *Trapped Within Welfare*, London: Macmillan.

Skenridge, P. and Lennie, I. (1978) 'Social work: the wolf in sheep's clothing', *Arena* 5(1).

Smiles, S. (1986) *Self-Help*, Harmondsworth: Penguin (first published 1859).

Smith, G. (1980) *Social Need: Policy, Practice and Research*, London: Routledge & Kegan Paul.

Soper, K. (1986) *Humanism and Anti-Humanism*, London: Hutchinson.

Spender, D. (1980) *Man-Made Language*, London: Routledge & Kegan Paul.

Statham, D. (1978) *Radicals in Social Work*, London: Routledge & Kegan Paul.

Stedman-Jones, G. (1971) *Outcast London*, Oxford: Clarendon Press.

Sterba, R. (1976) 'On character neurosis' in F. Turner (ed.) *Differential Diagnosis and Treatment in Social Work*, Glencoe: Free Press.

Sturrock, J. (1979) (ed.) *Structuralism and Since*, Oxford: Oxford University Press.

Szasz, T. (1963) *Law, Liberty and Psychiatry*, Glencoe: Free Press.

Thompson, E.P. (1963) *The Making of the English Working Class*, Harmondsworth: Penguin.

Timms, N. (1968) *The Language of Social Casework*, London: Routledge & Kegan Paul.

Timms, N. (1983) *Social Work Values: an Enquiry*, London: Routledge & Kegan Paul.

Titmuss, R.M. (1969) *Commitment to Welfare*, London: Allen & Unwin.

Towle, C. (1965) *Common Human Needs*, New York: NASW.

Turner, B.S. (1984) *The Body and Society*, Oxford: Blackwell.

Turner, B.S. and Hepworth, M. (1982) *Confession*, London: Routledge & Kegan Paul.

Turner, F. (1976) *Differential Diagnosis and Treatment in Social Work*, New York: Collier-Macmillan.

Ungerson, C. (ed.) (1985) *Women and Social Policy*, London: Macmillan.

Urwick, E.J. (1904) 'A school of sociology', in C.S. Loch (ed.) *Methods of Social Advance*, London: Macmillan.

Walby, C. (1987) 'Why are so few women working in senior positions?', *Social Work Today* 162: 10-11.

References

Walton, R. (1975) *Women and Social Work*, London: Routledge & Kegan Paul.

Wasserman, S. (1968) 'Ego psychology', in F. Turner (ed.) *Social Work Treatment*, New York: Free Press.

Watson, S. (1983) 'On the state – non state divide, another perspective', *Critical Social Policy* 2(3): 96-9.

Williams, R. (1961) *Culture and Society*, Harmondsworth: Penguin.

Williams, R. (1976) *Keywords*, London: Fontana.

Wilson, E. (1977) *Women and the Welfare State*, London: Tavistock.

Wilson, E. (1980) *Only Half-Way To Paradise: Women in Post War Britain 1945-68*, London: Tavistock.

Wilson, E. (1983) 'Feminism and social policy', in M. Loney, D. Boswell and J. Clark (eds.) *Social Policy and Social Welfare*, London: Open University Press.

Wilson, E. with Weir, A. (1986) *Hidden Agendas: Theory, Politics and Experience in the Women's Movement*, London: Tavistock.

Wise, S. (1985) 'Becoming a feminist social worker', *Studies in Sexual Politics* 6.

Wittgenstein, L. (1969) *On Certainty*, Oxford: Blackwell.

Wood, K. (1971) 'The contribution of psychoanalysis and ego psychology to social casework' in H. Strean (ed.) *Social Casework Theories in Action*, Metuchen, NJ: Sarecrow Press.

Yelloly, M. (1980) *Social Work Theory and Psychoanalysis*, London: Von Norstrand Reinhold.

Yelloly, M. (1987) 'Why the theory couldn't become practice', *Community Care*, 29 January 1987: 18-19.

Younghusband, E. (1951) *Social Work in Britain*, Carnegie UK Trust.

Younghusband, E. (1973) 'The future of social work', *Social Work Today*, 19 April 1987.

Zaretsky, E. (1976) *Capitalism, the Family and Personal Life*, New York: Harper & Row.

Author index

Subject index